23 YEARS,
23 MINUTES,
13 ANGELS

Biography of Short Stories
of an Ordinary Life in Ordinary Time
Enlightened by Extraordinary Awareness

Visions with Heaven-Sent Messages &
the Reality of Spiritual Conversion

Katherine (Kate) Hyland

 FriesenPress

Suite 300 - 990 Fort St
Victoria, BC, Canada, V8V 3K2
www.friesenpress.com

Copyright © 2016 by Katherine (Kate) Hyland
First Edition — 2016

ISBN
978-1-4602-7815-4 (Hardcover)
978-1-4602-7816-1 (Paperback)
978-1-4602-7817-8 (eBook)

1. Biography & Autobiography, Religious

Distributed to the trade by The Ingram Book Company

Dedication

In loving memory of my dear dad, Robert (Bob) Gough, a man greatly loved and dearly missed. "We will love you forever until the end of time."

Dad was an endearing man who started out by singing a song to me as a young child about "a dream." When his days on Earth finally ended, he left me with a "poem about a dream" filled with hope. In a loving letter, he wrote his personal thoughts, memories, advice and poetry. I can still hear his encouraging and inspiring words:

"Nothing beats you. You finish what you start."

"If I'm gone when you read this, I believe this isn't the end. I'll be waiting in a better place to see you again, at a later date."

May God give me the strength Dad, to endure to the end, when I finally meet up with you, in eternal life, for our astounding reunion.

Eternally yours,
Your forever loving daughter,
Katherine (AKA Kate and "your Kath")

August 2012 – Kate & her Beloved Father, Robert (Bob) Gough

IN LOVING MEMORY OF
Robert (Bob) Gough
August 30, 1928 – April 18, 2013

"Without a good woman, there would be no meaning for living today. Without children, there would be no reason to live for tomorrow. For we live on by being a small part of these, our children and grandchildren. And with this thought, death holds no fears."

- Unknown

Dedication:
Your Favourite Hymn
You Are Mine
By David Haas

I will come to you in the silence.
I will lift you from all your fear.
You will hear My voice.
I claim you as My choice.
Be still, and know I am near.

I am hope for all who are hopeless.
I am eyes for all who long to see.
In the shadows of the night,
I will be your light.
Come and rest in Me.

Chorus:
Do not be afraid, I am with you.
I have called you each by name.
Come and follow Me.
I will bring you home.
I love you, and you are mine.

I am strength for all the despairing.
Healing for the ones who dwell in shame.

All the blind will see, the lame will all run free,
And all will know My name.

Chorus:
Do not be afraid, I am with you.
I have called you each by name.
Come and follow Me.
I will bring you home.
I love you, and you are mine.

I am the Word that leads all to freedom.
I am the peace the world cannot give.
I will call your name, embracing all your pain.
Stand up, now, walk, and live.

Chorus:
Do not be afraid, I am with you.
I have called you each by name.
Come and follow Me.
I will bring you home.
I love you, and you are mine.

Contents

Psalm 23

A Psalm of David

The Lord is my shepherd,
I shall not be in want.
He makes me lie down in green pastures,
He leads me beside quiet waters,
He restores my soul.
He guides me in paths of
righteousness for His name's sake.
Even though I walk
through the valley of the
shadow of death,
I will fear no evil, for you are with me;
Your rod and your staff,
they comfort me.
You prepare a table before me
in the presence of my enemies.
You anoint my head with oil;
my cup overflows.
Surely goodness and love
will follow me
all the days of my life,
and I will dwell in the House of the Lord
forever.

Acknowledgments

From a small child, for as long as I can remember, I only ever wanted to become a teacher. For whatever reason, for whatever obstacles got in my way, it did not happen . . . until today.

To my beloved mother Ann, thanks for encouraging me to pursue this book. Your love will always light my way. You show your faith every day by continuing to believe in me. All children need a parent's faith in them. I'm so lucky and blessed you were my mother. My memories will keep you near to me, always.

To my husband John whom I met on a blind date on that fateful day, August **23**, 1985 (1+9+8+5=**23**). John always says, "You're one of the lucky ones, with deep faith, without any doubts. It will be your angel wings that I will depend on in Heaven." Meanwhile, on Earth, I will forever be indebted to you, John, for being my rock.

To my children – I love you more than life itself.

To my granddaughter Hailey with whom I have planted a seed. For one day you said to me, "Nana, I have a friend who also has visions. When I asked my friend why she would only tell me, she said, 'Because you are my trusted best friend, and I wanted to share them with you, but I don't care to convince anyone else, because I know what I saw." It's been amazing sharing life with you and watching you grow, Hailey, not only in size but in faith. Thank you for trusting in me to listen to and for letting me be a part of that miracle. I hope I'll be able to touch and educate the lives of all my grandchildren with these words.

To Kathy, a former colleague, who is now living in Taiwan with her husband and their daughter. You were the only friend with whom I confided the details of my first vision 23 years ago, and who believed me. Many years later, I found you half a world away through Facebook. I asked you if you remembered our conversation, way back then, when you told me, "You're so lucky. I would love to have a vision." This time you said, "I do remember that conversation! I totally believe in visions." Thank you, my friend, for listening and always believing in me. You have given me the courage to share my most intimate visions and private stories while assuring me my life was worth telling to the world.

To Judy ("Jude"), my saving grace. You held my hand and stood by me throughout my cancer journey. I wake up each day, thankful for my life, because I know somewhere, someone else is fighting for theirs. Having been on this journey yourself, you were my greatest mentor. I don't know what I would have ever done without you, my faithful friend. As I describe in my book, you surely "store up treasures in Heaven" every day.

To the late Robert Allen, who helped my dad through the last year of his life by becoming great friends through writing to each other and sharing dad's poems. Your "fourth daughter" misses your wit, your kindness and your presence. I pray you've now met my dad in Heaven.

Later, I learnt you were **13** years younger than my father—somehow no great surprise!

To my aunt Clare and Elaine (who inspired my last vision), my grandfather Herbert, my grandmother Rose, and my friends Pat, Norman, Janie and Julie, who have all called me an "angel." Your trust, prayers and belief in me keep me believing in myself.

To Carla, Karen, Russell, Lori, Charlene, Colette, Kay, Charles and all my many friends, who have since taken a true part of this journey with me, sharing, believing and encouraging me in this mission of faith. Thank you for always reminding me that you want to be the first ones to read my book.

To perfect strangers whom I came across and with whom I shared the makings of this book—the people who excitedly gave me their names and numbers to call them once it became published because they "couldn't wait to read it." As Jesus said in one of the most moving stories in all of Scripture, John 21, "Feed my lambs."

To my friend, Harla, for that amazing evening we spent together and for always admiring and inspiring my photography. You've been a true inspiration to my creativity!

To James and Dave, amazing long-time photography friends who were instrumental in helping me provide my photography for this book.

To my author friends Mary, Erica and Darlene who expressed the sentiments best described in the quote, "God doesn't call the qualified. He qualifies the called."

To my editor, many thanks to you for exposing the beauty and keeping sensitive to my words. I'm convinced God led me to you.

To God's **13** Angels who surround me and let me know I am right where I am supposed to be.

To my one Lord and Saviour, Jesus Christ, God's only begotten Son, who came to us as a baby, wrapped in light, born in the most humble of circumstances; who was sent on a rescue mission to save mankind from the penalty of sin; who died on the cross to pay that price for you, and me, and for all future generations. Ask Him for His help and forgiveness. He enriched my life with blessings and directed me with His perfect timing, for everything is about timing, in love and loss. He has changed my life for eternity. The Bible says, "For God did not send His Son into the world to condemn the world, but that the world through Him might be saved." (John 3:17).

To the day all creation is on bended knee, and the lion lies down with the lamb.

Editor's Comments

Thank you for the opportunity to review your unique book, and for sharing your insightful stories. You have written a wonderful and inspirational book that is filled with personal glimpses into the spiritual world, the kind that will resonate with many people who have suffered loss and illness. In particular, your discussion about spirituality and illness is very timely.

According to the National Cancer Institute in the United States: "Religion and spirituality have been shown to be significantly associated with measures of adjustment, and with the management of symptoms in cancer patients. Religious and spiritual coping have been associated with lower levels of patient discomfort as well as reduced hostility, anxiety, and social isolation in cancer patients and in family caregivers. Specific characteristics of strong religious beliefs, including hope, optimism, freedom from regret, and life satisfaction, have also been associated with improved adjustment in individuals diagnosed with cancer."

But, of course, your book is about more than healing from illness. It is about dealing with loss, disappointment, roads less traveled, and finding hope at the bottom of the well. It is also highly informative and well researched.

I once had a similar experience and whatever the explanation, my dream helped me; it eased my pain in a particularly dark period of my life. I thought immediately of this story when reading your book. Was it a vision, or just a dream? Was it a message from a family member who passed, or from God?

Many of us have visions that come to us in terrible times. We learn from them, if we are open to the messages they are meant to deliver. Some people dismiss them just as dreams, or they call them "intuition." But there is no doubt, in my mind at least, that they are very real. By sharing these stories, we can enrich the lives of others, and we can open up windows and doors, to let the air in, to clear away the dust and the cobwebs. Reading your book did this for me.

Many authors, like yourself, say they are "compelled" to write. This was not necessarily a path you chose for yourself; perhaps it is a path that has been chosen for you.

In *23 Years, 23 Minutes, 13 Angels,* you describe your personal journey and explain the ways you were able to make sense of your many challenges by following the paths set out for you in a series of spiritual visions. You also reveal the importance, and significance, of numbers that have served as signposts to guide you throughout your life. Through a literature review and a collection of stories from your own personal experiences, and those of others, you present evidence that Spirits and Angels are not just the stuff of novels—they are real. Your hope is that, by sharing your experiences and stories, you will be able to create a dialogue with others who have a) experienced visions themselves or b) are in search of a sacred path.

Your storytelling abilities are excellent. You are able to draw upon personal experiences to provide the basis for a spiritual-lesson book on how to live a better life, how to get through grief and great tragedy, and how to navigate the pain, suffering, and lack of hope. The characters you describe are well-drawn and are highly relatable. You have a talent for description that makes the reader feel that they are there with you along the way. I particularly enjoyed the tales of your travels to the Holy Land and places many of us will never see. Your journey is a textbook for anyone who wants to become more self-aware and sensitive to the mysteries of the spiritual world. It opens up a world of possibilities.

You have a lively and engaging writing style, which you use to great effect, particularly when describing harrowing personal events. I found your chapter about your personal health crisis both gripping and informative. On its own, it would make a great piece for a blog or even a first-person feature story.

There are many chapters that are very strong, and the writing is powerful. The chapter on your battle with breast cancer is a perfect example. You are unflinching in your description of your ordeal, and you are able to effectively engage the reader.

I tried to do this edit with sensitivity to your material, because I understand that everything that is here is here for a reason. I see editing as akin to gardening—the editor wants to take out any weeds, and brush, to expose its beauty. I hope I accomplished this for you. I try to be thorough, but only God is perfect.

23 Years, 23 Minutes, 13 Angels is a fascinating personal memoir that will appeal to readers who have embraced spirituality and made it part of their personal truth. It will also appeal to readers who are searching for answers during difficult times in their lives.

The stories are engaging and uplifting!

You may note that I finished the edit on September **13**.

All the best,
Your FriesenPress Editor

Introduction

Faith is being sure of what we hope for and certain of what we do not see.

—Hebrews 11:1

Twenty-three years is how long I've been having visions. **Twenty-three** minutes is how long the doctor in the recovery room said they did compressions, as they worked on my dad to try to save him from a cardiac arrest, seven hours after a life-threatening aortic aneurysm surgery.

The day of his funeral, Tuesday, April **23**, **2013** was the day God told me I was now working for Him, as I rushed over to my Bible and confirmed Psalm **23** in my mind: "The Lord is my Shepherd, I shall not want."

When I said it out loud, I felt goosebumps appear, which I now call "angel bumps"; I knew from past experiences these had always been my sign of "my truth." They are the mental and physical reaction I feel when my **13** angels are guiding me to the highest good, and it happens to me all the time.

So by "my truth," I mean "the feeling of trust I'm having in that moment."

My angel bumps don't necessarily confirm I'm about to experience an unpleasant event, but their appearance could mean yes, I'm on the right path towards leading someone, or something, out of potential danger later on. I know I'm on the right path, and usually, I'm feeling that what I'm doing is unselfish, loving and right. The chills are like confirmation from a Higher Power; they tell me to follow my gut feelings, to follow my faith.

Sometimes, they are very strong. Sometimes they start on the top of my head and radiate down my spine. These stronger ones are rare and are even harder to ignore when they happen. They are alarming indicators that tell me I'm on track and make me feel certain I'm not wrong.

In the Gospel, we hear Jesus say, "I am the way, and the truth, and the life. No one comes to the Father except through Me." I'm sure many of us tend to think of "the truth" as a set of doctrines or dogmas or ideologies. In the Gospel, "the truth" is referring to a person, and that person is Jesus – the One in whom we put our trust. He is the way to Heaven, eternal life and the Father.

The day of my first vision was no different than any other day. But it was a day when I knew something had changed me forever. From there I started my research until it happened again, during the onset of my cancer, many years later. On the day of my father's funeral it all came together. It all started to make perfect sense and I finally knew what I was supposed to do with the last **23** years. God's timing is always perfect. Thanks be to God!

I once read this: "A *coincidence* is defined as the accidental occurrence of events that seem to have a connection."

With God's direction, I'm about to share with you what seems to be something that is beyond coincidental.

When I've shared these stories with my friends, they have told me, "You're so lucky. You're special. I wish this would have happened to me."

Others said, "I always knew you were a very special spiritual person who seemed to have something important to share. I got this feeling from the first time I met you."

Recently a teacher friend told me, "You are such an inspiration, you have been through so much and just hearing about your journey makes me look at life with different eyes. You certainly have been blessed with a rare gift."

They all said, "You need to write a book and give hope to the world and I'm looking forward to it!"

I'm not a Scripture scholar or theologian. I'm not even a crazy person who should be locked up somewhere. I'm a normal, sensible person with good judgment who has been blessed with several visions and some astonishing coincidental experiences. Two of these experiences happened after I was diagnosed with breast cancer; another, I believe, came to me to prepare me to lose two special souls in my life within a four month period; and yet another, to reaffirm I had nothing to fear as He was there to increase my trust.

I've led what one would consider a normal life, likely not too much different from yours. I'm a wife, mother and grandmother who recently retired after being employed with the same company for nearly 40 years.

In 2009, my cancer journey began. Cancer, together with my visions, put me in a new place; I would never return to the old place again.

Writing down my thoughts in a stream of consciousness helped me to translate the knowledge I received through my "dreams." It helped me change my priorities and redefine what was really important in my life.

My profound encounters with Christ changed me forever.

I know there will always be those who read my stories and go on the "spiritual attack." They will try to find other explanations. I knew that when I entered that first library

23 years ago. I'm not here to argue or convince; I'm only here to share how it all played out for me and how it affected my life.

In the Bible, throughout history, God spoke in many different ways, so why not now? It made me take notice and believe that if we keep our minds open, we will realize nothing is a coincidence. I feel we have been called to be keepers and defenders. It's just that I have found the narrow gate. I have presented it to you as it was presented to me, unfiltered, not watered down.

Society allows philosophers, poets and song writers to put labels on what things mean. Why can it not be a higher world speaking to us wherever we are? This new world I find myself in defies all arguments between religion and science—between belief and unbelief. My advice to you is *simply listen*. When I became involved in raising funds for research through the Cancer Relay and the Run for the Cure, I felt I was only scratching the surface, that I was only helping people in one of the normal ways that we have become accustomed to helping people.

I've learned, in almost every situation, that we as individuals can't do everything, but we can do something. I knew finding the words, piecing the puzzle together, and jumping off the high board by telling my story might be considered controversial and speculative. I needed to find some path beyond "getting involved for a cause." I assure you, becoming an author, and bringing the message of His glory into the lives of others, was not in my original plan. But then again, neither was it in my plan to have a potentially fatal illness at the age of 51.

This is not a story you've already seen published after an NDE (near-death experience). It's not a story meant to convince you that I went to Heaven and returned with revelations. My story is a living experience. It's been in the making for **23** years. In the beginning, I didn't even know what I was supposed to do with it.

As a result of my journey, my faith has been deepened, and I stand before you as a conduit to help you become more conscious of your presence, and purpose, here on Earth. I will show you how you can prepare for your re-entry into the spirit world after physical death.

It's very easy to believe in things when you see them, but it's much harder to become aware and be able to recognize the things you cannot see. This is a learning process otherwise known as *faith*.

A child once shared with me two very simple stories.

First she was sitting at a table, and she held up both of her hands and said, "Here are my hands!" She then took both of her hands and put them under the table. "Now because you cannot see my hands, does that mean they are not there?" she asked.

Secondly, the same child asked me, "The Bible, what does it stand for?" "Does it mean basic information before leaving earth?" (Don't you love kids who see things through such innocent eyes?)

People also need to be more concerned about other people and their needs and not be motivated by greed and material achievement. Actions speak louder than words.

* * *

On the morning of my father's funeral, I awoke at 2:00 a.m., my mind filled with information and thoughts that I knew I needed to share with a wider audience. The thoughts came into my mind so fast that it made me shake as I scribbled them down on notepaper. I really can't explain it. Now, as I read it all back, I'm amazed at the words I was given.

Six months earlier, I had begun to read all these spiritual books that kept mysteriously landing in my hands. It was just before my husband, John, and I decided to take a pilgrimage trip to Israel.

I now realize it was a sign for me to share my experiences and life stories by writing my own book to help others to believe that our spiritual life is much more important than our physical life.

The problem was I didn't consider myself a writer. So that is when I set out to find a writer until I was told the Bible itself was written by people just like me.

When I reflect back to my childhood, I remember having a great imagination. When I became an adult and had to face all the realities and obsticles of the real world, I no longer had the same creative ability yet I can describe to you my visions and my intense feelings in precise detail.

Part-time professional photography has always been a passion of mine. I started my own photography business and photographed weddings for over 13 years. I was awarded several ribbons and received honourable recognition including a CAPA - Canadian Association of Photographic Art award as I entered several photographs in contests and fairs. I also became an active council member in a local photography club. In 2007, while I was on an overseas vacation, I took the photo that is the cover of my book, years before I even decided to write this book. I immediately knew this particular photograph would have a higher purpose, because it captured my heart and soul to the inner core.

It is my deepest desire that the profits from the sale of this book, be donated to the charitable organizations of my choice. In Colin Powell's words, "Giving back involves a certain amount of giving up."

By doing God's Will, I am happy to give up anything to serve Him. I am grateful for what God has bestowed upon me; I was the one who benefited the most.

In the pages of this book, I pay tribute to the loving memory of my father, whose undying love will live on. As for me, I hope my truths can change lives. More importantly, I hope they can help change yours.

Chapter 1
You Tell Me Your Dream,
I'll Tell You Mine

Worship the Lord with gladness; come before Him with joyful songs. Know that the Lord is God. It is He who made us, and we are His, we are His people, the sheep of His pasture.

—Psalm 100:2–3

As I walked toward the pulpit, trembling, I passed the urn containing the earthly remains of the dearest man I will have ever known, a person whom I deeply loved and respected my entire lifetime.

My parish, and the funeral home, referred to it as a "celebration of life" instead of a funeral, but I now felt lonely, sad and not joyful. A part of me had just died. Somehow, I felt, on this occasion, that Dad was the only one who was now celebrating because he was the one who had returned to the glory of God's world. Death still remains one of life's greatest mysteries.

Five days earlier, I had been the last person to tell him I loved him. Three hours after those last words, I was standing in the recovery room with my mother receiving the worst news of my life. My mother had just spent 67 years married to the man and was about to be told "God needed him more."

It seemed hard to believe. That same day, my father had survived his elective aortic aneurysm surgery. But seven hours into his recovery, he suffered a cardiac arrest, and he was taken from our world to His.

God had sent his most loving and gentle angels to collect Dad's soul to take him *before us* to live in Heaven with Him forever more. Dad is now with his past loved ones having a glorious reunion.

My faith told me all this, but on that day, I was still processing the deep loss we were all feeling. I felt as if I would never recover, that my life would never be normal again. Death leaves you devastated, and it's impossible to ignore the sadness and hurt. Inevitably, each of us gets to know that unavoidable, horrendous emotion.

During my mourning period, I learned a few lessons. One was "Nothing ever stays the same."

Things we take for granted can be taken from us permanently, and suddenly, and we're forever changed. It's true: in life, there are no dress rehearsals. In Alan Bennett's words, "Sometimes there is no next time, no time-outs, no second chances. Sometimes it's now or never."

I knew it would take time to overcome the feeling of overriding sorrow. I also knew that life brings sorrows, and with sorrows come tears. I knew it wouldn't always be that way. According to Isaiah 25, "The Lord God will wipe away the tears from all faces." Our sorrows are temporary. Our joy will be eternal.

I also knew to celebrate the memories and the blessings you did have. How lucky I felt to have something that made saying goodbye so hard.

But it was hard. As I proudly stood facing the congregation, in my Dad's honour, I recited only 5 per cent of what I could have said about a man with the most triumphant of spirits.

I had been lucky. God had answered so many of our prayers and had granted us so many blessings. I knew how lucky and blessed we had been, but all that somehow didn't make that day easier.

Earlier the same week, I'd had a serious conversation with God. I knew if Dad had lived to be 100 years old, it still would not have been an adequate amount of time. There is never enough time, and you are never ready to let go of someone you love so much. I reminded myself of James 4:7, where the apostle instructs, "Submit yourself, then, to God." There are moments in life when we just have to turn to Jesus when our pain is too great to bear ourselves.

Something told me it was time to stop feeling as if I were making deals and asking God for favours. I had to start thinking as God does, not as a human being. Deep down, I had known there would come a day when God would call my father home. I knew I had to accept God's Will, as I had asked Him in prayer to give me the wisdom to help know His Will and know His heart.

There comes a time in life when you must get out of the way and trust God has picked "the perfect window" and put you in the proper place, at the proper time, to allow His glory to shine through. I've also learned that the prayers we often refer to as unanswered can be either God's Will or the answers to someone else's prayer. Either way, they both have the ability to become miracles.

For example, my mother asked God if He would grant Dad one or two more years. Meanwhile, Dad prayed that if it was his time, he would go fast. I prayed that whatever was God's Will, so be it. I knew I couldn't continue making deals; things were coming to an end. Later, my mother mentioned her prayer had not been answered, and I replied "No, but Dad's prayer was."

I continued the eulogy. "Where do you begin to sum up 84 years and tell about a great man in a few sentences?"

If the people at the service knew my dad, I realized then, they already knew the answer. He was a devoted husband, loving father, wonderful uncle, kind brother, great friend. He loved children and animals. He was gentle, trustworthy, compassionate, kind and loving, and he gave to so many charities. Those of us whose lives he touched were truly blessed. Every photograph showed the warm and loving smile he gave to everyone he knew.

My dad was the youngest in his family. After his mother had six miscarriages, three children were born. Dad was the youngest of nine. I found the story of his birth incredibly fascinating and rare. My grandmother's water never broke before he was born. He emerged into this world in what was called the *caul.*

To be "born in the caul" simply means a child is born with the amniotic sac, or membrane, still intact around the body. When a baby is in the caul, the sac balloons out at birth, covering the baby's face as the body emerges from the mother. The baby is in no danger of drowning, as it is still being fed nutrients and oxygen through the umbilical cord, and the baby will not take its first breath until the face emerges from the fluid contained in the caul. The caul is harmless and is easily removed by the doctor or midwife. When my grandmother delivered my father, apparently the attending nurse had never witnessed this type of birth before, and her reaction quite frightened my grandmother until the caul was removed.

A child born in this way is known as a *caulbearer.* It has been calculated that caulbearer births may be as few as one in 80,000 births. Such births are quite rare, and they hold special significance for the child born in such a manner.

11

Many stories and myths have been written about the caul, and many of them are erroneous. Regardless, it's quite a phenomenon.

The positive myths that are associated with being born in the caul have a physiological basis, in that the baby is not exposed to potential infection until the membranes rupture. Therefore, being born in the caul carries an almost zero risk of neonatal infection being transmitted during the birth. Especially in the past, before antibiotics, this would have increased the likelihood of a newborn surviving the first month.

Midwives are more likely to allow babies to be born in the caul. Some midwives believe allowing children to be born in the caul has spiritual significance; others simply think nature should be allowed to unfold as necessary, especially as there may be some physiological benefit to being born this way.

In medieval times, the appearance of a caul on a newborn baby was seen as a sign of good luck. It was considered an omen that the child was destined for greatness. Dad would agree that it was more than good luck. His life was "blessed by the grace of God."

Gathering the caul onto paper was considered an important tradition of childbirth. The midwife would rub a sheet of paper across the baby's head and face, pressing the material of the caul onto the paper. The caul would then be presented to the mother, to be kept as an heirloom. In my Scottish grandmother's case, I was told the nurse who delivered my father here in Canada asked to keep the caul, as creepy as it sounds, after my father was born.

Over the course of European history, a popular legend developed suggesting that possession of a baby's caul would give its bearer good luck and protect that person from death by drowning. A caul was highly prized by sailors.

Medieval women often sold these cauls to sailors for large sums of money; it was regarded as a valuable talisman.

Legends also developed for the caulbearer. One popular legend says such a person would be able to see the future, or have dreams that come to pass. The Scottish believe a child born in the caul will become fey, or psychic. One British belief is that the child will travel its entire life and never tire. Another myth associated with the caul states that they are made from the nightgown of Jesus, and everyone must respect the person as he may become a saint someday.

It is also thought that if twins are both born with cauls, they are marked by an angel and their souls are shielded.

In the Icelandic culture, a child born with a caul was considered to be special: they would go through life with a faery companion, a shadow figure known as the Fylgiar. The Fylgiar serves this person, and the person also serves it while asleep or when making deliberate astral projections. This faery can be heard in the person's home, banging and knocking around.

The Fylgiar's most disturbing responsibility is to warn its human companion of his or her own death, at which time it becomes visable. The condition of the Fylgiar at the time of the sighting indicates what sort of death it will be. A mauled faery means a nasty, painful death, while a peaceful one means a calm, painless death. The Fylgiar continues to live on after the human dies, but it accompanies its person to Valhalla, the Nordic Land of the Dead, where it remains until the human soul is comfortable and accepting of his or her demise.

My mother once told me a disturbing story about a time when my young father dove into Lake Erie from a pier in Port Stanley. She said she remembered him staying under the water an incredibly—and dangerously—long time. She recalled the feeling of fear that came over her that something had gone terribly wrong with the initial dive. As many anxious minutes passed, he finally came up to the surface with a big smile on his face. Then she remembered the mysterious myth of the caul known for protecting from death by drowning.

As I was sitting up, late at night, writing my dad's eulogy with a friend, our fridge kept making a knocking sound. At one point, it became really loud, and I said to my friend, "What's up with that?" We'd been in this house eight years, and the fridge had never acted like that before. It wasn't till I read an article about the caul that it made me wonder!

For his part, my father constantly warned my mother of his death. She was so disturbed by it that she started calling him a *crepehanger* which is defined as one who takes a pessimistic view of things. She then warned him to keep positive and encouraged him not to worry about his health issues.

My brother and I would hide his cigarettes but it was not until his older brother died of a heart attack at age 41 that he quit smoking.

It wasn't until Dad was having trouble cutting grass and walking along the beach in Florida that he began having angina attacks. At age 66, he underwent a quadruple bypass. After the surgery, the heart surgeon explained that his heart had grown a vein around it, making its own natural bypass. She commented she had never seen this before, and she said this would have never have happened had he not quit smoking.

Dad held my brother and me responsible for saving his life by hiding those cigarettes. Some may say it was the good luck of the caul, or perhaps that his soul was shielded. Although I found all this to be very interesting, I believed it was another blessing from the grace of God.

In Dad's late 70s, he underwent surgery to insert a stent in a failing artery. His heart surgeons warned of the high risk, but with faith in the surgeon—and His Creator—Dad decided against the odds, and bought himself six more years. Thanks to God and modern medicine, Dad lived to be twice the age of his brother.

Dad was fighter. Before his last surgery, his faith told him God was in control. He loved life and his family even more. He lived his life this way: always giving of himself, sharing his wisdom and talents, always doing good for others, and always showering his love on us every day. We were never rich in money, but we were a family rich in memories. The happiest people don't always have the best of everything; they make the most of everything they have. This was our dad, from day one to the last day he was given.

Happiness is said to come to those who cry, those who hurt, those who have searched and those who have tried, for only those who have experienced all this in life can appreciate the importance of people who have touched their lives. Unfortunately, the saddest moments in your life arrive when the person who gave you the best memories now becomes your memory.

One day, during my cancer recovery, my dad showed up at my front door with flowers because he knew I was having "a down day." The card read, "Keep positive, you will beat this."

His smile confirmed his deepest desire to help me. He always kept me hopeful, encouraged me and reminded me to trust in God. This was at odds with my doctors, who had other ideas. They provided the statistics and the variables in a fancy chart that showed me my odds over the next 10 years.

One day, Dad and I had a deep conversation, and he said, "I guess I will never know if you beat it."

Without even thinking or blinking an eye, I blurted out, "Yes, Dad, you will know. You will see me either sooner or later." This, of course, meant sooner in Heaven if I didn't beat the cancer and later in Heaven if I did beat the cancer.

Suddenly, you could hear a pin drop. Neither of us could bear the notion of losing the other, but we both knew our God was the God of miracles, and we both believed the impossible could happen every day.

As a child, I remember my dad teaching me the Lord's Prayer. He would repeat it line by line until I had it memorized. He always made lessons into games. The Lord's Prayer is truly a perfect prayer given to us by the King of Kings with the certainty that Heaven and eternity is the true reality. Have you ever truly thought about its meaning?

It starts by acknowledging God as the Father and blessing His holy name. We then ask not that the kingdoms of men be built up but, rather, that God's Kingdom will come to us. Then rather than asking for our will, we ask that God's Will be done. His Kingdom already exists in Heaven, and His Will will be done, for nothing can stop the fulfillment of all prophecy.

It then ends with four petitions: asking that God will feed us, forgive us, not lead us into temptation, and deliver us from evil. For those times when we're not sure what to pray for, or how to pray, this prayer should always be on our lips.

I had asked Dad if he remembered teaching me the Lord's Prayer, but he hadn't. We had thought that dementia was stealing his memory, but now we understand that his condition was brought on by a lack of oxygen to the brain. When I reminded him how he taught me this prayer, tears rolled down his face as he realized he had left an important imprint on my life right from the start.

The first song Dad ever taught me was a song he used to sing to me as a young child. It was called *I Had A Dream, Dear.* It wasn't until I started writing this book, which was inspired by his passing that I realized my story had started with a dream given to me by Dad, that it consisted of dreams and visions sent by God, and that it ended with a dream given to Dad by God.

This is the beginning of that song. I'd like to inspire you with it by sharing it with you:

I Had a Dream, Dear

I had a dream, dear. You had one, too.
Mine was the best dream
Because it was of you.

Come, sweetheart, tell me,
Now is the time.
You tell me your dream,
And I'll tell you mine.

I had a dream, dear.
You had one, too.
Mine was the best dream
Because it was of you.

Come, sweetheart, tell me,
Now is the time.
You tell me your dream,
And I'll tell you mine.

Chapter 2
Childhood

When you were born, you were crying
And everyone around you was smiling.
Live your life so that when you die,
You're the one who is smiling
And everyone around you is crying.

— Unknown

It was an ordinary street with ordinary families. I was born into an ordinary life. The year was 1958 (5 + 8 = **13**) and (1 + 9 + 5 + 8 = **23**). It was a simple time back then. The Depression was long over, but the war had left its imprint, along with bitter memories. Still, people were starting to move forward with their lives.

The lot our house sat on was a wedding gift from my grandparents to my parents. My grandparents lived next door and this turned out to be a wonderful gift to our childhood.

Our house itself was prefabricated, and they called it a Kernahan. I think Kernahan was the name of the company that made it, but my mother always led me to believe it was because the main characteristic of this type of home was that the kitchen was in the front of the house. (My parents soon changed that detail.) "Prefab" modules were basically assembly-line houses, and those who bought them touted their benefits: they were cheaper, better constructed and more environmental, and folks could move into them more quickly.

I didn't care what type of house it was, but I particularly adored living next door to my grandparents because I was able to see them every day. I remember walking into my grandmother's kitchen, with its high ceilings; the entire space was filled with the smell of fresh bread baking.

For many years, my grandfather used to come into our house to wake us up for school, prepare our breakfast and get us ready for school in the mornings. My mother would have all the dishes and our clothing set out.

The only thing my Papa wasn't prepared for was my demands about how I liked my toast in the morning. One day, it had to be cut in two; another day, cut in four; and there were other days it just had to be folded. My grand-mother later commented how he "just couldn't understand the difference, but she had to have it the way she wanted or, she wouldn't have anything to do with it!" I guess either I knew what I wanted, or I was just trying to test an old man's ability to accept change!

Everything else for me pretty much flowed well every day—except on one St. Patrick's Day, when my mother had forgotten to leave out my green dress. That was the day Papa insisted that I be a little Scotch girl instead. I think this was the one and only meltdown I ever had with this sweet man whom I loved so dearly.

Now, my brother never argued with Papa about any-thing. He pretended to go along with what he said but also did what he wanted anyways. My mother used to insist that my brother wear a raincoat on the days it rained, but my brother hated his raincoat. Rather than argue, he would put it on and pretend he was walking to school. Once he thought no one was watching, he would run back and place the raincoat in the milk delivery box. That seemed to work well for him until one day, Papa caught him!

I'll always remember going over to my grandparents' house on July 20, 1969 to watch NASA's Apollo 11 Lunar Module land Neil Armstrong, the first person to set foot on the moon. His first words after stepping on the moon, "That's one small step for man, one giant leap for mankind," were televised to Earth and heard by millions. We owned a television of our own, but we went to my grandparents' house because they owned a "coloured television." I soon found out it didn't matter, because the pictures from the moon were in black-and-white! I think it was a good excuse, as we just loved being in my grandparents' presence. Children who grow up with the luxury of having grandparents in their lives are truly fortunate. To experience and be around that unique love can make life-changing memories. It is usually their first involvement with the elderly.

I also loved our neighbourhood and the times in which I was fortunate to grow up. Those were the days we rode our bikes without bike helmets and rode in cars without seatbelts. Those were the days when our lives were sun-kissed, and we would play outside all summer with our friends. We would wind up the days by playing a neighbourhood hide-and-seek game at the corner light post. It was great fun, and we knew it was time to go in when the streetlights came on. My mother was a born-worrier when it came to her children. Thank goodness for Daylight Saving Time, which extended our playing time until we would go home, all played out, in time for a bath to wash our dirty hands and bruised knees. There weren't hand sanitizers back then, but on the occasional off day, adults would threaten to wash our mouths out with soap!

My brother and the boys in the neighbourhood decided to build a go-cart out of scrap parts of wood and wheels from someone's old lawnmower. We would all pile in and ride this gem down the hill, on the sidewalk, until it reached the end, where it veered off to a dirt path. The go-cart didn't have brakes, so either it would slow down on its own, or we would lean to the one side and dump ourselves out as it hit some weeds and bushes. I remember hearing, "Don't cry now!" This was all before they built an apartment building in this location. Innovation was slowly moving into the neighbourhood, changing its look and our freeway.

I really had a shine for an old neighbour named Mr. Edwards, who lived next door on the other side of our house. In some ways he reminded me of my grandfather. He once found a skateboard in his overcrowded garage, and he gave it to me. My brother and the boys in the neighbourhood all came up with valuable trade-items "a girl might want" in hopes I would give up the skateboard to them. They thought the skateboard would replace the go-cart and be the new vehicle of travel. I drove a hard bargain, but I obtained some great school supplies and the beginnings of my stamp collection. That skateboard, with its peeling green paint, got repainted in new fluorescent psychedelic colours of purple and black with the design of a footprint on top. They obviously wanted to make it their own.

On blazing hot summer days, we would drink from the garden hose and run through the sprinkler. On our simple sidewalk, we would open small Kool-Aid franchises and sell lemonade made from real white sugar. On a really lucky day, we would be taken to the public pool or given money to visit an ice cream truck that would find our street; its driver would ring its bell to call out to all his patrons. My favorite Good Humor was Strawberry Shortcake.

Many years later, my parents put a small above-ground swimming pool in our very own yard. It was always filled with that delightful sound of children screaming and splashing. My parents always loved all our friends being at our home. I never learned to swim past the dog paddle. Obviously, I wasn't born in the caul!

There was a man in our neighbourhood called Steve who seemed to have an overgrown property. He had a grapevine trellis in his backyard and huge bridal wreath bushes in the front of his house that never seemed manicured. He always was kind and friendly to each of us, and now when I think of it, I think he just loved the sights and sounds of children happily playing.

To us, Steve was a curiosity; we noticed he only had one arm. I attributed his yard jungle to his 'handicap'. Rumour had it he lost his arm during "the war," which we really knew nothing about. At the time, the only thing I knew about war was that my grandfather went to it. No one ever seemed to want to talk about it. I just figured war wasn't a happy place, so why would anyone want to know more about it?

Perhaps this was the reason why Steve loved the sound of our happiness as much as we loved to play dress up and simulate weddings by shaking his bridal wreath bushes to make confetti. We would wear my mother's old high heels and old dresses, which were pretty long on us.

I wonder now, who exactly did we marry? I guess we didn't need husbands back then, but we did have baby dolls, so I guess we were the ones who invented single parenthood. Life seemed a whole lot easier than it is today. Maybe our imaginary husbands were always at work, or at that terrible place called war, or maybe they didn't want to come home to eat the real-dirt mud pies we served on our small china dishes.

None of the children in our neighbourhood were overweight, and that is no surprise. Playing hopscotch, high jump, hula hoop and skip rope to our hearts' content was the first natural and organic health and exercise program available. For a small adventure, we made up games with tennis balls and our mothers' old stockings as we recited verses I now recall to be more like nursery rhymes.

We would ride our bikes everywhere. We rode them to a truck-trailer called the bookmobile. Imagine a library on wheels! We rode them to the nearby curling rink's recreation hall, where they held conventions and wedding receptions. The very minute we heard the cars honking, we knew it was a wedding party arriving at their dinner venue. We would leap on our bikes and peddle ourselves senseless to arrive at the best viewing place to catch a glimpse of the wedding party and the bride. I'll always remember my very first sighting of a bride emerging from the car. I actually thought I saw my first angel's reflection.

I remember my brother and his friends would play with small firecrackers, cap guns, BB guns, and bows and arrows. Wow, how safe was that in the neighbourhood?

I can still see my mother hanging clothes on clotheslines; she had long poles to prop the lines up so the clothes would hang higher into the breeze. We always liked to use these same poles to stick in the chain-link fence to play high jump.

I attribute my creativity today to making the most of all the free and natural resources I had available to me as a child. Life seemed simpler in a lot of ways back then, and life seemed so unsophisticated.

There were no such things as PlayStation, Nintendo, Xbox, laptops or tablets. There were no video games, video movies, DVDs or VCRs. There wasn't anything called Blu-ray or Netflix. Our television, which was set into a wooden console cabinet, only went up to **13** television stations, and it required this funny looking aerial that stood, like a sentinel, on the roof of our house. All our neighbours had one.

There were no Black Box converters with multiple channels or split or flat screens. There wasn't any surround sound or boom boxes, CDs, cell phones or iPods. There weren't any personal computers, Internet, Facebook, Twitter or chat rooms. The only square box we had was an Etch-a-Sketch or a chalk board!

Today, we have at our fingertips more options than at any point in human history, which we can use to find a deep connection with someone. It makes me wonder: with so many ways to connect through technology, why are so many people frustrated with their lives?

Back then, we walked outside and sought out our real friends to chat and play with instead. Everyone who needed to reach us was usually with us, and if they weren't, we could connect with them using the telephone in the house—which was attached to the wall. On this telephone, you had to dial the telephone number instead of pushing buttons, and the person who answered wasn't a machine.

Back then, the only interruptions were on a "party line" on your telephone (multiple customers were connected to the same phone line). Today, interruptions are normal, and distractions are constant on everything from the cell phones you carry on your person to sales pitches on every means of telecommunication.

Today people multi-task and we race from one activity or appointment to the next. If only these interventions could be used to help create perfect work–life balance. By that, I mean finding a time to work and help, a time to play and, most importantly, a time for restful prayer. We are so hurried and worried we often forfeit our richest blessings and neglect our greatest personal opportunities. If only we could realize that we need to put extra effort into all of our endeavours. I once heard that whatever we invest most of our time into, it's usually what means the most to us. And this, my friend, should equal people! Praise God, I didn't have all these things to keep me preoccupied and make me ignore my incredible grandparents.

Back then, we ate white bread, real butter and bacon, and we ate less processed food. We ate at the kitchen table with our mothers and our fathers and our siblings, and we learned our manners. We rarely ever ate out at a restaurant. In fact, the only restaurant I can recall going to was a drive-in restaurant. They brought burgers, foot-long hot dogs, and "chicken in a basket" out to our car and placed them on a tray that was hooked onto the window glass. As a real treat, we drove to outdoor drive-in movies, where we wore our pajamas, and our parents brought blankets, sodas and homemade popcorn. Our cars didn't have seatbelts, movie systems or airbags then, either!

To this day, as I drive under a certain underpass in my city, I think of my dad. It was there he always drew my attention to the radio in the car losing connection and going off. It became a game. Today, it brings tears to my eyes every time I drive under the same underpass. Back then, there was time for interpersonal games. Many times, while sitting in the car, waiting for my mother to return from an appointment, we played *I Spy with My Little Eye*. How many of you even know this game, or would think to put down your toys for fifteen minutes and demand interpersonal time with your kids?

The best time was summer weekends or vacation, when we drove to the beach as a family. My mother would fill the cooler with sandwiches, fresh carrot sticks and celery, homemade cookies, and soda pop. My dad would prepare the inner tubes and foldable lawn chairs. We would take the dog, and we all would pile into the car with our bathing suits and towels; it was the greatest anticipation there possibly could be. I knew we were really on the way to the beach when we drove by a particular house that had its own private pond, which stood on the outskirts of the city. That house isn't there anymore. In its place stands a high-rise seniors' building.

As an adult, I now realize that the lake was only 75 kilometres away, but as a child, it seemed to take forever to get there. It was a popular family beach, located on the southeastern shore of Lake Huron in the municipality of Lambton Shores, Ontario, called Ipperwash Beach.

We knew we were in the final stretch of our journey when we reached the last road, which was covered with soft beach sand. You could hear the effect of the wheel wells filling with sand on the road that led directly into the lake. We strained our eyes searching to view the blue lake ahead. As we reached the end of the road we looked for the big wooden Casino and General Store building on the left corner. It was the last landmark announcing we had arrived at the beach! I can still remember the distinct smell of the building and the sound of the creaking wooden floor boards as we walked in to order the best maple walnut ice creams cones *in the world*! The ice cream melted immediately in the hot sun, unlike some of the ice cream today, which contains palm oil and so many other preservatives and unhealthy additives.

Dad drove the car straight onto the beach, where families parked their cars, one after another, directly on the lakeside. By the time we arrived, the dog was slobbering down the window. He, too, could smell the lake and hear the seagulls squawking. Dad would take a corkscrew device made for dog chains, screw it into the sand and then leash Rebel not far from where our sand pails and shovels were laid in preparation for the construction of the sandcastle and moat.

I still remember those days; in my mind, it was as close to Heaven as I could have ever imagined. Since then, I have driven to this same beach, but today there are many changes. The big wooden Casino and General Store building is gone, as it burned down many years ago. You can no longer drive or park on the beach next to the shoreline with its rolling waves. When I remember those precious days, there isn't anything I wouldn't give to have one moment back there again with my family and that rambo of a dog who wrapped his sandy dog chain around my ankles till I cried.

In winter, my dad would build us an ice rink in our driveway or backyard. I think I actually learned how to ice skate before I learned how to walk. And skating for me was so much easier than learning how to swim!

I remember watching Dad through the frosted paned glass window; he'd be out there in the cold evenings, holding the hose in the dark, making the ice rink perfect for us. My mother would make me wear mittens on strings, but the most frustrating part was when our dog would leap at my mittens and try to pull them off me. (It was hard to make Rebel understand I was attached to the mitten leash!) Regardless of all the abuse I took from that beagle, I loved him so much. After the heartbreak of his death, I started bringing home an array of stray dogs and cats with kittens who all had an incredible unconditional love for children.

The best part about this neighbourhood was the houses across the street that backed onto factory property. My friend's house happened to be one of those houses. She was one of five children. We would crawl under the fence at the end of their yard, and in the summer, it lead us to a haven of natural adventure, complete with tadpoles and frogs, rocks and mud, long grasses and forts. In the winter, it provided us with hills to toboggan down and a natural pond to ice skate on. It wasn't uncommon for us to eat our supper with our ice skates still on our feet, with newspapers underneath us, so we could get in "one more skate" before darkness fell.

My friend's backyard also provided healthy snacks for the summer. It had a pear tree, a cherry tree, rhubarb, fiddleheads, raspberries, red and black current bushes, and even gooseberries. We ate fruit first, making the candy at the dime store "the luxurious occasional treat."

The other night, when my husband and I went for a walk, we talked about the fact that we now never ever see a child out after nightfall—or out after school, for that matter. How life has changed with computers and child pornography fears. Whatever happened to children playing road hockey as our boys did?

The world has changed in such a way now that children don't know how to be creative using the simple elements in life. They don't know how to learn to deal with disappointment because now, everyone makes the baseball, soccer or hockey teams. Parents bail children out of situations instead of making them atone for breaking the law.

The very fact prayers cannot now be said in school, unless your child attends a Christian school, is strange to me. And I often wonder how many parents kneel down by their child's bedside at night to teach them how to pray or pray with them. Some of my fondest memories are of my parents praying at bedtime with me as a child and of sharing prayer time with my own children.

Tough love taught our generation well. It has produced some of the best problem-solvers, athletes, inventors and risk-takers. We were right in the middle of an explosion of innovation, new ideas, breaking records, and rock and roll. We had freedom, failure, success and responsibility, and we learned how to deal with it all. Today, many of life's failures are people who don't realize how close they are to success when they give up; instead, they resort to even more negative options such as suicide, divorce or substance abuse.

We attended church on Sunday and never had to make a choice between shopping or church, because church was the only facility open; it wasn't open for discussion. We came home and spent time with those we loved, visiting grandparents and talking to parents over a home-cooked meal.

We believed God was watching over us as we thanked Him for all the small blessings we had in our lives. Family values were cherished, and we had face-to-face conversations. Today it's not even uncommon to see someone walking across the street "texting" someone from their cell phone oblivious to everyone else around them including cars!

I like to look someone in the eyes and pay attention to body language. It's about really listening to someone and having them also listen to me. It's about respecting someone enough, and valuing your time with them, and giving them your undivided attention. It's about being present and living the moments, because moments slip away and are gone forever. Those moments become irretrievable. That's reality.

When have you given another person, or even Mother Nature, your full attention? Taking in the fresh air and the beautiful landscape around you can be grounding, head-clearing and mood-lifting, and you will find the world is stunningly beautiful if you open your eyes and use all your senses. You can learn a whole lot about life by observing the awesomeness of nature. Being a photographer has taught me this well. When was the last time you stopped to marvel at the smallest exquisite treasures all around you? Have you even noticed the diamond glints on snow? How about the dewdrops on a buttercup or the intricate spider webs that have been spun on a boxwood hedge? When was the last time you gazed at the stars or laid on the green grass and stared up at the cloud formations? Try it—you can still do it with a glass of wine, although you may fall asleep!

In Luke 10, Jesus says the Father is "revealed to the childlike." Being childlike means children believe what their parents tell them, and they trust their parents to take care of them. Skepticism doesn't come until later in life.

So, in the spiritual life, being childlike means we believe and trust what God says. He will take care of our every need and, as a loving Father, He will never disappoint. It also means to know how to slow down, see the people and world around us, and be present with a sense of appreciation and wonder. Let the heat help you appreciate the cold. Let the dry spells help you appreciate the rain. Let the darkness, and the cloudy days, help you appreciate the sunshine. Notice the stars, the constellations, the sunrises, the sunsets and the seasons. Notice the colours, the tides, the birds and the changing habits of the animals and wildlife. Begin today to be more Earth-conscious before your eyelids close forever. Notice the symbolic meanings hidden in everyday things and notice light around you even when others see darkness.

What I really have a hard time understanding is why God always gets blamed. When the acts of God happen in our world today in the form of hurricanes, tornados, forest fires, mudslides, flooding, volcanic eruptions, severe thunderstorms, tsunamis and earthquakes, and when things escape our control and tear up our world, we are the first ones to ask God why He is letting this happen. In almost the same breath, we ask Him for help. Why is it that when there is nothing left but God, you find out that God is all you need?

The knowledge of my visions tells me the growth of the universe is constant, but the violence, hatred and angry emotions that have been let loose in the atmosphere by the collective thinking of mankind is causing the natural disasters. These disasters affect us all, including the plant and animal world. It has to stop, or the unbelievable will become commonplace. The planet itself is punishing us, not God. It all works together. Save your energy to wage war, because you will need it to sustain yourself against the natural elements to maintain equilibrium.

Each one of us is responsible for terrorism, economic turmoil, rampant immorality and harming the planet with chemicals. The fallen nature of the world we live in will ultimately result in hardships, but people make their own choices. God isn't making them do these things, nor is He stopping them. This is similar, on a personal scale, to when we have struggles in marriages and family—burdens of medical issues, trouble in a job, an accident, her husband walks out, his doctor found cancer, or they lose a baby. Many times, the universal adversities of living life are at work, as all life comes with problems.

Being a Christian does not make you immune to freedom of choice or the freedom of choice for others. Every time, when we turn on the news, the world is full of trouble and pain, and there is conflict on a global scale that can be exhausting and overwhelming and make us afraid.

In John 16:33, Jesus says, "In the world you will have tribulation." He also says, "Do not be afraid," and this is written in the Bible 365 times. Jesus was fearless because His love was perfect, and "perfect love casts out fear" (1 John 4:18).

Is that not a daily reminder from God to live every day fearlessly? Remember, the gift of faith is given by God. There is no room for fear there. Not being afraid of death only comes from faith. The more we put our faith in the power of Christ by replacing our fears with trust in Jesus—that He has our backs and He has a perfect plan for our lives—the less our fears will control us. In troubled times,

31

just know that the Universe has your back and that everything is going to be all right. If you're not there yet, trust in hindsight, and you will understand. Your higher good is being supported, always. More on this is in Chapter 20.

Once, I heard a story about the space shuttle. While it was orbiting the Earth, one of the astronauts commented on how beautiful our planet looked from above. He also said he couldn't see any divisions of countries or anguish or tensions between nations. We all looked "as one" from up there. Yet on Earth, we separate, divide and conquer through power, religion, money and politics. We sometimes even desensitize ourselves to the rest of the world's problems as a mechanism to survive and stay above the fear.

My father used to quote the Bible by saying, "You reap what you sow." What we must remember is that God is all merciful and all loving, and He should never be blamed for negativity because that is a by-product of humankind. Religion has many complexities, and God too often gets blamed by humans in the world. Our existence on this Earthly plane is meant for learning, to gain perfection and experience Divine love, not reward. Eternal life is our reward, and it is assured to us if only our hearts truly embrace God's love. Meanwhile, Satan has been trying to separate mankind from God's love since Adam and Eve.

As a young child, I tried to be friends with everyone and lived by the motto "We are all from different worlds, but it is love that binds us." For years, I wrote to pen pals all around the world, from Korea, England, Denmark, the Philippines, Malaysia, Pakistan, India, Abu Dhabi, the United States of America, New Zealand and Australia. Some pen pals came and left, but one friendship, in particular, I can proudly say has lasted for over 40 years. She has visited Canada four times, and I have been to Denmark three times.

I'll never forget my first time going to Denmark. It was a year after her husband had died suddenly of a heart attack. Her father later shared with me, that the very thought of my coming to visit her helped to keep her focusing onward. Of course, I had to fly the first leg of the journey, but I arrived at her small town by train. The second time by plane and the third time, as a port of call on a cruise ship! It's true: if there is a will, there is a way!

We have experienced and navigated a lot together throughout the years—the dating scene, college, our parents and families, marriage, children, pets and losing pets, divorce, remarriage, trips, holidays, unemployment, re-employment, retirement, and even serious sicknesses and death.

We now call each other "sisters," and we are always planning the next get-together. Our children have met and all know each other, so we have already paved the way for the next generation. Thinking back, I can't ever imagine having not shared my life with her, even though we were worlds away. Our friendship has been life-changing, and our lives were made rich by our relationship, as we've helped each other through many trials and tribulations. I love her dearly. I have learned really good friendships are rare, and it has been a real blessing for us to have both found each other. We call ourselves "sisters by choice."

In her words:

"Dearest Kate

Even though you are far away, I feel that you are so near to me.

I read your story, and I listened to the hymn that your Dad loved. I just sat there crying at work, early in the morning, no one else was there yet. What a beautiful song. You are amazing, I know nobody else like you. You move my heart so much. I can't express my gratitude enough that you came into my life many years ago.

I love you, and I wish you were here so that I could hug you."

No matter the distance between us, God has been the cement.

My husband and I have been so fortunate to have been united with other wonderful people we now call friends through our church, cruises, and visiting and staying in other countries.

We really are so much the same, and too often, we don't tell those we love and meet that we love them, even when these people share the intimate, most special moments of our everyday lives. Share with others how good God has been to you. Hug often, and smile more. Count these friendships and magical meetings as blessings in your lifetime. This is what St. Paul means when he says, "Bear witness to the Gospel of God's grace." Sometimes you simply need to slow things down, take notice and simplify your life. Then you can sit back and watch the power of God work in your life.

Chapter 3
Growth

Forgiveness is giving up the hope that the past could have been any different; it's accepting the past for what it was, and using this moment, and this time, to help yourself move forward.

— Oprah Winfrey

I can't change the direction of the wind, but I can adjust my sails to always reach my destination.

— Jimmy Dean

When I think how much I love my loved ones— my father, whom I couldn't love any more than I did; my mother, whom I love so dearly; my husband, my one exceptional love; and my children, whom I love with every fibre of my being—I think about what the Bible tells us. Put Him first in our lives, for His love must be so great in comparison to the love we have here on this blue ball we call Earth. When we are able to do that, our love for our loved ones grows even greater as a result.

One of the reasons why I believe I stopped seeing the visions for quite some time was because, for a time, I had lost my way.

For all of us, life gets in the way, and circumstances make you question your faith and your purpose in life. People also have a huge influence on your life, even if you don't admit this. But the struggles in your life can pull you in the direction of Jesus as much as they can pull you in the opposite direction.

Honestly, there wasn't ever a time I didn't believe in God, and I knew He still loved me, but I chose to disconnect and go on with my life, keeping His presence at a distance. I found myself talking to Him less, praying less, attending fewer public prayers, thanking Him less and generally moving forward in my life with the feeling that He wasn't there and there wasn't a need for Him to be close by. There seemed to be too many do's and don'ts in Christianity that didn't appear relevant in modern culture anymore. So over a span of time, I attended church sporadically and let the wind guide my direction without the aid of a compass.

There was a lot going on. It was a dark time for me, as it followed a difficult childbirth in a deteriorating alcoholic and substance-abusive five-year marriage. Although the relationship wasn't physically abusive, the toxicity made it become dramatic and emotionally damaging. Eventually it led to a third person "that understood him," and this brought on the dissolution of my first marriage.

Soon after my divorce, I remarried, and my new complete happiness taught me an all-embracing forgiveness for the past. I learned that the only way to be happy again lived in the ability to forgive and let go of the pain of my previous unsuccessful marriage.

As I moved on, I assumed a new role of becoming a stepmother to two older children who no more wanted me as their mother as I wanted my first marriage to end, so this new life also brought with it brand-new challenges for us all.

With that came a series of job losses and family struggles, complicated by the birth of a fourth child whom we had wanted and planned. Even though we felt blessed, life in general with four growing children seemed like a whole lot of work and confusion. I think today it is referred to as the modern-day family, the blended family or in some cases the dysfunctional family!

Anything that made it worthwhile meant work and couldn't be accomplished in a rush, or without failure. So, being young and determined, we did our best and soon learned that plummeting was part of life, but getting back up again was learning how to live. This had to be as difficult as it was to practise the teachings of Jesus. It takes practice, diligence and persistence, but the benefits are eternal. The lesson I did learn throughout this growth was "Faith doesn't make things easy. It makes them possible" (Luke 1:37).

Don't get me wrong, remarrying was the best thing I did, but trying to correct the mistakes in between was where the real struggles and challenges came into play. The small details of your life are what really matter in a relationship; it is not the mansion, the car, the property or the money in the bank. These create an environment that can be conducive for happiness, but they cannot give happiness in themselves.

I still remember the advice we were given the day we were married with three children already in tow: "Don't let your children ever come between you" and "Always remember how you feel today."

I also found myself going to church more "for my kids" and going through the motions of making sure my children were raised with good family values and were seeing strong spiritual practices (although I admit that at the time, I left a lot of the religion practices up to the school teachers). We just continued on, planting and watering, trusting the growth would eventually come. A great rule of patience is "Plan in decades, think in years, work in months, and live in days."

During all this time, I never stopped, deep down, believing in God. But at the time, I knew I was doing what I thought was right but not necessarily doing things from a faithful servant standpoint. I tried to forgive, repent and learn from the past so history would not repeat itself. But I started to ask the many questions: Why did this happen? Why me? Why now? What did I do to deserve this? Why doesn't it happen to someone else? Where is God? Sound familiar?

It can also come at a time of crisis or when you are faced with unexpected adversity. For me, I call this "the time I lost my way," and although it is hard for me to admit to anyone, let alone put it to print in this book, I know I sometimes hated my life because of my failures. Those feelings can occur in everyone's life but just because you are struggling, doesn't mean you are failing. Every great success requires some type of worthy struggle to get there. Looking back, it now all seems like a lifetime ago.

The one good lesson I did learn well was not to carry the past anger from my first relationship into my next relationship. Even though my ex-husband continued to make my life miserable for many years, deep down, I forgive the past and put up with the weekly squabbles over the details of my daughter. By doing that, I was able to embark on a journey to find love again, be in love, live in love and truly be blissful in my second marital relationship. Also, wishing my first marriage never happened was not an option, because I was given a beautiful gift. For that important lesson in my life, I was given a daughter.

It also wasn't until I wrote this book that I realized the 13s were with us all along. While raising four children, my husband lost his job twice. But now looking back from retirement, I see he worked with three different companies, all a total of **13** years each! All I can say about that is "For everything is in God's time."

In Ellen DeGeneres's words, "When you take risks, you learn that there will be times when you succeed, and there will be times when you fail, and both are equally important." This is how we learn, but it's normal to simply question everything, including God and faith in general, and sometimes you end up thinking, "What is the use?" As you go deep, have you ever asked, "How do I even know if Heaven is for real?" Sometimes the hardest part of being a Christian is taking things on faith, including experiencing the bad things that happen in our lives. It is only then, by recognizing the bad times that we can truly appreciate the good times. Have you noticed that sometimes these bad things put us directly on the path of the best things that will ever happen to us?

In my case, I may have not felt He was close by before, but now I've learned, and witnessed, that Jesus is all around us, and He shows up in our lives every day. The real question is, do we see Him?

Once I fully understood God's Will, it then became abundantly clear. God, in His great mercy, has another plan—a better plan. Not trusting His Will could be why we have failure, which becomes a lesson in itself; thus, when God closes a door, he'll open a window. In Helen Keller's words, "When one door closes, another opens. But we often look so long and so regretfully upon the closed door that we don't see the one that has opened for us." The open door is usually the circumstance forcing us to move forward! (Helen Keller was the first deaf blind person to earn a university degree.)

My life has consisted of myriad medical maladies from a very early age. Between the ages of four and eight, my sleep disturbances began in the form of very active sleep-walking. This started with sleep talking but then escalated from quiet walking around the house to agitated attempts to stand on a dresser to picking giant gold rings off the bedspread to putting my boots on in the middle of winter and nearly "escaping the house."

I understand now that sleepwalking typically occurs when a person is in the deep stages of sleep. In my case, sleepwalking was associated with incoherent talking with my mother as she would return me to bed. My responses would be slow, and if I didn't wake up, I wouldn't remember anything. But if I awoke, I often remembered the event. My mother told me my eyes were open with a glassy, staring appearance, but I was indeed asleep.

Between ages four and eight, four fearful and trans-formative incidents occurred. In the days when seatbelts weren't mandatory, I was jumping around in the backseat of the car while my parents were driving home from my cousins' in our family car. I suddenly started choking on a hard candy that I'd been given just before we left our cousins' home. I still remember my mother shouting to my father, "She is choking!" Immediately my dad brought the car to a screeching halt, got out and picked me up by my ankles while my mother pounded me on my back until the candy popped out. Today, people would likely be quick to accuse my parents of child abuse, but this was a glorious act performed by two frightened and loving parents to save the life of their child.

Shortly after my parents performed this life-saving maneuver, like many of those born in the Forties and Fifties, my childhood memories included being admitted to hospital to have my tonsils removed. In a study of surgical decision-making, in the mid-1960's, it was found to be the most common childhood surgery aimed at treating chronic throat infections due to the premature discovery of penicillin. The high-ceilinged ward crammed with rows of cribs to prevent us from escaping, is not the only nightmare etched in my mind.

While waiting to be taken to the operating room, someone pushed my stretcher from the hallway outside the operating room into a small storage room where the laundry staff kept supplies and pressed uniforms. They all seemed friendly enough, but at four years old, I didn't know enough to question why I was suddenly taken out of sequence and misplaced in the hospital! It wasn't until the two children who were scheduled to be operated after me, came out of the operating room before me, did my mother experience a complete melt down.

Before I went into the hospital, I remember my father telling me if I didn't cry, he would make sure there would be a Chatty Cathy doll waiting for me. This was really an anomaly because up to then, Santa Claus was the only one who gave us toys. Chatty Cathy was a pull-string "talking" doll that was manufactured by the Mattel toy company from 1959 to 1965. The doll was first released in stores and appeared in television commercials beginning in 1960. She was on the market for six years and was the second most popular doll of the 1960's after Barbie. (I never owned Barbie. I actually had a "Margie" Barbie-type doll that my mother purchased with food stamps from the local grocer). It wasn't until years after when I had children of my own, did I confess to my father that "I didn't cry when they lost me but I did cry in the operating room." I will always remember his moving response. He said, "It's okay. I knew you would cry. I only asked you not to cry, because I knew if I saw you cry, it would make me cry."

The third fearful incident happened at age five when I was skipping with my skipping rope at recess at school. A stray baseball escaped a baseball diamond and hit me in the head, knocking me out cold. Those were the days when they brought you to the school nurse's office, let you sleep it off and then sent you home alone with a note! To my parents' horror, they discovered that evening, after X-rays at the hospital, that I had suffered my first concussion.

The fourth frightening incident happened while my parents were installing a new kitchen window in our house. A neighbourhood friend of my brothers came and asked if I could accompany her to the variety store. The variety store was located one street over from where we lived, and it was considered the "busy street" as it was on the bus line. My mother agreed to let me go with her, but she instructed the older friend to promise to leave me sitting on the bus stop bench as she crossed the street. In hindsight, a guardian angel must have been whispering in my mother's ear that day, because for some reason, my mother didn't want to give permission for the girl to take me with her across this street.

As the friend turned to come back to me, I watched in horror as a car hit her and she went flying several feet. My scream could be heard a block away. My mother and the other girls mother, came rushing to the location.

Summer for this friend turned out to be miserable, in a body cast with a bar between her legs. As for me, I remember only moments before begging her to take me across the street with her. Fortunately, I was spared injury or disaster that fateful, grateful day. Bringing her flowers and cookies was a beautiful and blessed compromise for what could have been a terrible fate for both of us.

At eight years old, I suffered a traumatic injury to my back as a result of a horrible toboggan accident. While going down a hill on a wooden toboggan, which seated five comfortably, we flew over a snow covered tree trunk; I flew backwards, chipping and damaging vertebrae in my lower spine. I crept off the toboggan and crawled all the way home, and although the medical details to me as a child were foggy, a small van would come to my school two times a week and take me to the Crippled Children's Centre for therapy treatments. It is only now, many decades later, that I realize the seriousness and repercussions of this accident and the life-long issues I would later endure. Today that hill has been ploughed down and a new subdivision is in its place. If only it was as simple as to go back and replace the life-long pain with something else.

Up until this age, my only exposure to death had been on the television. At the age of four, I clearly remember sitting alongside my mother as she wept. Unfamiliar to seeing my mother cry, it was upsetting to me. I asked, "Why are you crying mommy?" Her reply still remains ingrained in my memory and it seems like it was just yesterday. "Because, President John F. Kennedy has been shot and this is his funeral", she said.

By age 10, I had emotionally suffered two major deaths in my immediate family. My dad's brother died of a sudden massive heart attack, and two years later, my grandfather, who was my best friend, died. They said my grandfather died of cancer, but after my uncle's death, I'm pretty sure the cause was a broken heart. As you will learn further on, my grandfather was one of the people who influenced my early life. Together we shared a special bond. It was a loving, devoted and intimate relationship.

Six years later, when I was 16, Dad rushed me to the hospital in the middle of the night only to find I had developed kidney stones. Nine years after that discovery, the kidney stones appeared again while I was carrying my first child.

During my childbearing years, my two pregnancies were anything but textbook. I had preeclampsia, AKA toxemia, which is a serious complication of pregnancy associated with the development of high blood pressure, edema (swelling), and protein in the urine; untreated, it can cause death. Worldwide, it has been estimated 5 to 14 per cent of pregnancies are complicated by preeclampsia—in the U.S., it's 3 to 6 per cent—but my odds seem to have always fallen into the low percentile.

Two more concussions followed later in life. My second concussion happened while we were on vacation with our children camping at the Grand Canyon. I slipped in the shower at the campground we were staying at and banged my head so badly that the only thing that could be done to bring me back to consciousness was to turn on the ice-cold water full blast. After that, with my goose egg and vertigo, we bolted for home with great speed.

The third concussion occurred in a car accident, which I will describe in Chapter 9. Today, as a result of all these head traumas, I occasionally get migraine headaches, and I also get ocular migraines, which produce auras, sparkles or cloudy vision instead of an actual headache. By this time, I think I could have been a self-taught nurse!

Years of physical trauma were followed by the emotional anguish of family struggles that included divorce, job and financial struggles, and other losses.

Finally, while celebrating my 50th birthday on a beautiful cruise vacation, I slid down a black coral embankment while photographing pictures on an island. Luckily, the only thing I lost was my bladder.

By the time I got home, medical results indicated my uterus was prolapsed, and a uterine hysterectomy was strongly recommended. Six weeks later, the pathology report revealed "the cells were changing," and the doctor surprisingly said, "Had this not happened, you likely would not have been around to celebrate age 60."

My parents used to say, "Why does that girl have to get everything?" Well, it's not *everything* until you get cancer, which I did eventually manage to get, too, only four months after the hysterectomy news. This is what I called "my domino effect." No wonder, I liked cats—I was beginning to think I must have been given nine lives like a cat! Thank God for all the angels nudging me along. Problem was, for the next 16 months, I felt like I was caught in the eye of a hurricane and there was no way out. But it's okay, because I'm alive today to tell you my amazing story.

Today, I'm reminded that spiritual lessons can be learned more easily through illness. When God sends us suffering, He does it only to strengthen our spirits so we'll be strong enough to fight off Satan, who wants to destroy us, and to make sure that one day, we will be able to bask in the glory of His presence. Satan must be too close and threatening to me, as God surely must be giving me a huge shield to strengthen my spirit from him. It is with that thought that I accept my sufferings; they seem to be worth their pain. After all, Jesus himself accepted our sufferings to teach us the virtue of patience in human illness and disease, and if He could do it, I could, too.

Attitude is everything. I once dreaded celebrating "another birthday," but today I celebrate each birthday with joy that I'm still here! I think differently than I once did, when I look at nursing homes, for that would mean I'd survived the odds and made it that far.

I'd also like to think one of His gifts to me was "compassion," for me to know the agony of pain and suffering myself. It allows me to recognize the condition in others so I can seek to help them in their struggles. A prayer I once heard said, "May all who suffer pain, illness and disease realize they are chosen to be saints, and know they are joined to Christ in His suffering for the salvation of the world, who lives and reigns in you." To keep our focus, we must be reminded that our sufferings are minuscule compared to our Lord's human suffering 2,000 years ago.

The advice my husband John has given me is to "never let go of the anchor." He continued, "The waves will get rough, but they will eventually settle down. As long as we keep holding on together, we will be okay." I kept focused on what he said: "Building this together, and withstanding this storm forever, for I knew we could make it if we were heart to heart." I think, at the time, he was referring to our marriage, but in Hebrews 6:19, it refers to hope as the "anchor of the soul."

It's the same with God, if you think about it. Some theories in life are simpler than you allow them to be. Jesus said you must love your life and you must carry your cross and be worthy to follow Him. For we all have hardships, or crosses to bear, at some time in our lives. It may be sickness, death; for some, it's job loss or relationship troubles. For others, it may be a particular propensity to sin—lust, anger or pride. Sometimes God will take away your cross, but be assured there will be another waiting around the corner. And when the next one comes, we must pick it up and carry it as well, always relying on the strength of Jesus to help us along the way. Every time I've picked my cross back up and regained my focus on Him, my life has taken astounding turns. He really is with us. Believe it.

The Gospel reading from John 17 is often called "The Lord's Prayer," but it is not the "Our Father" prayer that often comes to our mind. This Lord's Prayer refers to the time when Jesus prayed to His Father for all believers to become one. As there had always been a division within the body of believers, He referred not only to the believers in His presence or those from the first century but to all believers for all of time. "I pray not only for these," He said, "but also for those who will believe in me through their word, so that they may all be one." His unity prayer was for you and me and for every Christian throughout time.

Even among well-intentioned believers of yesterday, or today, there can be doctrinal differences and differences in practice, but I believe this oneness for which Jesus prayed can be explained in one four-letter word: L-O-V-E. We don't always have to agree with one another, but if we were all united in L-O-V-E, the world would be a much better and more peaceful place.

Life is so much about the choices we make and, because of those choices, we have consequences. Did you know you get to choose your eternal destiny? You do every minute of every day. We can choose to obey God (life), or we can choose to turn our backs on Him (death). The choice is ours. Quite simply, God doesn't send anyone to hell. We are the ones who have the gift to choose and make our own decisions. Although God wants us to use our free will for the good, we can choose death or life, the curse or the blessing, and we do this by exercising bad judgment or choosing eternity by having the grace to want to live forever in His care.

Everyone has always told me I march to the beat of my own drum and that I am "a rebel," yet I always stick to my values and stay true to myself while being empathetic to the suffering of others. With a generous heart, I'm driven by the search for meaning, and I have a passion for culture and religion.

I'm a deeply spiritual person who thrives in a stimulating environment where people question their existence and devote themselves to a higher sense of being. I see life as an adventure, whether I'm spending time in a bustling international market or meditating in my quiet garden, enjoying the interaction of the birds.

My family is my world, and it's lonely without them. My loyalty to those who love me is endless. I try to keep myself nourished, and dancing, and I try to never let the world get me down. I am not perfect, and I often feel life has been a feat. Attitude can be infectious, and love is everything. We all want to be loved. It is part of our DNA. Our deepest desire is to be loved.

I think the most difficult work, for me, is in helping others see what I see and explaining to them how to obtain the faith as I do. I'm not a priest, minister, deacon, Scripture scholar or theologian. I'm only a person with a soul with faults and attributes, like you.

You see, I believe faith begins with the *knowledge* of what it is that should be believed. For example, if you know the Gospel of Christ according to the Scriptures, you have the knowledge; however, it is possible for you to know what the Gospel is without believing it to be true. To reach the next level of faith, you must also believe it to be true, which is called *assent*. But this is still not enough for salvation, which takes us to the third aspect of faith: trust. *Trust* refers to a personal commitment to and reliance upon an object of faith. In salvation, the sinner accepts these facts are true by knowing that Jesus suffered and died in love for us and that He rose again from the dead; our spiritual mistakes or sins are freed by His blood.

On a personal level, I continue to pray for my own brother daily, that he one day will be able to trust what I have known and have been shown. For him, I can see a big mountain. Could you also be on the same mountain?

He seems to carry anger, and he struggles with religion and the church by looking at it only from a business side, which is the version the world created. He fails to see God beyond this and is not forming his own relationship with the energy force: God himself.

All I can see today is a person who doesn't even realize he is doing God's work. I see his moulding cracking as I hear his stories of travelling south to Third World islands, three times a year, to spend some sunny days but never without a care package for the less fortunate. I hear him say he fills his suitcase as he brings t-shirts, sports hats, children's school backpacks and even women's sanitary napkins to the underpaid and overworked hotel service people who work in the tourist industry. They have such limited access to the simple necessities that we have readily available to us here in North America.

He boasts how these island natives go out of their way to care for and treat tourists well, and for me, his response translates into "love." At the same time, I'm seeing and hearing how my brother is giving back to them in ways he knows, and he feels they are receptive, appreciative and deserving. I also see what a good father he has been to his two boys, both now grown; he loves dearly. If loving our fellow man isn't an act of God's work or living God's love, I don't know what is.

I always tell him, if and when the day comes that he wants to talk to me about "this God" and invite Him into his heart, I will be there for him. My dad's last wish was that my brother wouldn't wait to get to know Christ until his final hours. I pray every day that the Lamb returns long before then.

Unfortunately, the world has molded our thinking; many believe the cross is foolishness and all religion is irrelevant. But those of us who are incorporating the power of God's work into our daily lives see souls being taught, and saved, without even knowing it.

I also believe community prayer is really effective, even though we are all truly on our own individual journeys. I leave this question to my own brother by saying this: "When you reach the end of your journey and reflect upon your life, will your soul 'soar in freedom or agonize in strife'?"

I strongly believe our time here on Earth is meant for each of us to learn. Although I am now a practising Roman Catholic, I also believe organized religion (not Christianity) was created on Earth, not in Heaven or by

God. I view this along the same line as different languages. Although I understand the practice of swinging incense and its symbolism "of the prayer of the faithful rising to Heaven," I struggle with some traditions, rituals and cultural differences. After all, Christ and the Virgin Mary were Jews. What remains strong and true is my core relationship with God himself.

Hinduism, Buddhism, Christianity, Judaism and Islam are the five major religions in the world. These religious groups over the past few thousand years have shaped the course of history and have had a profound influence on the trajectory of the human race. Through countless conflicts, conquests, missions abroad and simple word of mouth, these religions have spread throughout the globe and have molded geographic regions in their paths. But although we often inherit our religion, I think it's wonderful that we are able to change heart and move to another religion to find our level of spiritual realm, if we so wish. With each step, we can weed out things that aren't relevant to us and decide where we need to be.

Some days I lose confidence, and I question if one religion is better or more correct than the other. In fact, I am often reminded that religion is a business unlike anything else in this world. Religion has created much distress in the world, and I don't accept this was God's intention.

When God is rounding up His sheep, He will simply know the hearts that love and truly believe in Him. Religion is merely a means of structure. It shocks me the amount of blood and death and torture the Bible portrays. There are a lot of brutal and ruthless people in the Bible, but I believe it all portrays growth, and we should honour God's commandments, learn the lessons of the Bible and love God with an open and sincere heart—AKA Divine Love. As for me, I follow my faith basically because I believe in the basic core values written in the Apostles' Creed.

For those of you who don't know it, these are the words:

I believe in God,
the Father Almighty,
Creator of Heaven and Earth,
and in Jesus Christ, His only Son, our Lord,
who was conceived by the Holy Spirit,
born of the Virgin Mary,
suffered under Pontius Pilate,
was crucified, died and was buried;
He descended into hell;
on the third day He rose again from the dead;
He ascended into Heaven,
and is seated at the right hand of God the Father
almighty.
From there He will come to judge the living and the
dead.
I believe in the Holy Spirit
the holy catholic church
the communion of saints,
the forgiveness of sins,
the resurrection of the body,
and life everlasting. Amen.

Remember what Paul and Barnabas taught about how it was "necessary for us to undergo many hardships to enter the Kingdom of Heaven" (John 14:27). Jesus promises the Holy Spirit, a promise of spiritual truth: "Peace I leave with you; my peace I give to you. I do not give to you as the world gives. Do not let your hearts be troubled and do not be afraid."

Peace and hardship are like oil and water. How can these two coexist? I'm sure you have met someone who seems to have such peace, even in the midst of some of the worst storms in life. These are the people who know what it means to trust God and to believe He is in control; they are in tune with the Spirit. Seeds have been planted, and the

Holy Spirit has watered them. People often refer to this as "inner strength" because that's what makes sense to them, but yes, you may say, "Who knows what's really going on?"

This reminded me of my first vision, when I felt indescribable happiness and incredible peace that was far greater than any peace this world could even begin to comprehend. Peace is not the absence of trouble, but the presence of Christ. Today, when things are going well for us, we feel at peace, but it is a transitory peace. It isn't until the storms happen that we see how Jesus's peace overarches everything, including the storms. And the storms will happen, but with God there's always a rainbow waiting. There is a day of disaster for each and every one of us.

Life is hard, and it is never perfect. We're not in control; it is only an illusion. He is in control. But we need to "act as if it were impossible to fail" and "let go, and let God." When we let go and let God, worry disappears. So why do we worry in the first place? Why don't we relax and let life happen without incessant worry and micromanagement? I believe it is because we know we don't have complete control over every situation, or perhaps we simply fear the unknown. Jesus talks about worry and how we need to live for today, as worry will never add a single moment to your life.

Although this takes great practice when this happens to me, I have learned to replace worry with prayer, asking for the confidence to trust in Him. This trust was demonstrated in my first vision, which I'm about to share with you, in which He is holding my very being. I've found when I actually visualize Jesus physically holding me, I have been able to truly receive the deepest faith. The definition of *faith* means taking God at His word with full confidence—both His promises and His warnings—and acting accordingly. For me, this is where faith and trust in God become "one." Paul says, in Romans 10:17, "So then faith cometh by hearing, and hearing by the word of God." Biblical faith is not an "unquestioning belief that does not require proof or evidence." This is not a blind leap of faith. It is an intelligent, holy reaction to the wondrous words of God!

In Matthew 9, Jesus speaks again and again about the need for faith. It is at that point that He is able to heal two blind men. Jesus asks the blind men, "Do you believe that I can do this?"

They answer Him, "Yes, Lord."

He then says to them, "Let it be done for you according to your faith." It is then they both receive their sight, which exemplifies their great faith coming directly from the Lord Jesus. In times of weakness, trust can make Christ's healing power complete in all of us.

The first letter of St. Peter reminds us we will "suffer through various trials." Often we are even tested and are tempted by our own disordered desires. But this suffering is not worthless, as it will help us to "attain the goal of faith, the salvation of your souls." It is our faith in God's plan that make miracles happen.

Chapter 4
My First Vision

*And it shall come to pass in the last days, saith
God, I will pour out of my Spirit upon all
flesh: and your sons and your daughters shall
prophesy, and your young men shall see visions,
and your old men shall dream dreams. And
on my servants and on my handmaidens I will
pour out in those days of my Spirit; and they
shall prophesy.*

—Acts 2:17–18

It was like any other night in our household, an ordinary end to an ordinary day. Everyone had shared good conversation at the dinner table, and we had family time preparing lunches for the next school day. Baths were given, and clean pajamas were put on. Prayers were said, and lights were put out. The odd child would find an excuse to make one more trip to the bathroom for another drink of water, but other than that, there was nothing too earth-shattering.

I completed the last motherly chores long after my children were safely tucked into bed, and then, I retired to bed.

I said my prayers, thanking God for keeping my children and everyone one else in my life safe and healthy and for providing all that we had. I kissed my husband goodnight, and the house then fell into darkness for yet another day.

I had fallen asleep, only to be awoken abruptly a few hours later. The next thing I knew, I was sitting bolt upright, my eyes wide open, and the first words that blurted out of my mouth were "If that is anything like dying, I'm not afraid." I awoke my husband, who was lying beside me, with these words, and even though I knew he heard me, he turned to me to confirm what I had just said.

"What did you say?"

I thought to myself, "How many dreams do you ever actually see yourself in?" (I'll tell you how many: none! It is because you are in them and not viewing them from the outside.)

I sat there for a moment and knew this was far beyond any dream I had ever experienced. It was an inexplicable experience that I can recall in detail, to this day, over **23** years later. This first vision, I strongly believe, was a Divine vision given to me by God; it was the most pivotal moment of conversion in my life.

This vision was not so much about what I saw; it was more about what I felt. What I felt were all the negative, mortal feelings and emotions we as human beings are capable of feeling on this Earth. They are referred to in the Bible as "the darkness." I did not feel these dark emotions individually, on their own; I felt them all at once—fear, envy, doubt, jealousy, hate, grief, anxiety, selfishness, confusion, humiliation, malice, loneliness, depression, despair, hopelessness, destitution, sadness.

It felt as if every negative emotion were coming together in the precise *last second* of my life. These were all the feelings of negative energy we possess as part of our human weakness. It was like Satan was casting his heavy darkness upon me. I then felt a close, dark tunnel surrounding me, and I felt as though I were travelling faster than the speed of sound—by tornado speed—forward! I couldn't see anything in particular, but it was then I heard and felt a release, a bursting sound. I had made it past, or through the darkness, but I couldn't quite tell how, other than the fact that a feeling came over me like no other feeling I had ever felt before.

The closest description I can give you is that I felt indescribable contentment, a PEACE magnified by a million, billion and zillion. When I looked up, I saw the brilliance and intensity of surrounding beauty and purity radiating a soft, warm, beautiful golden glow of light shining around and surrounding Christ and from within Him—a light that was rejuvenating and overwhelming but not to the point it made you squint or was sore to the eyes. It had a healing, calming presence and was peaceful to the soul. It was like an all-consuming deep love filled with joy and confidence. It was ever so powerful, and loving, that my consciousness didn't know how to comprehend it; it was such a calming sense within my soul. I knew then it was God's light, for I knew God's love could heal all souls. It had to be—for it was of the greatest magnitude I could have ever imagined. There was nothing ordinary about it.

Christ was in a sitting position, holding me across His arms. It reminded me of the famous masterpiece of the Renaissance, the marble sculpture *Pietà* (pea ay TAH), carved by Michelangelo Buonarroti when he was **23** years old. The sculpture, which is now housed at St. Peter's Basilica, Vatican City, Italy, shows Mary holding and grieving over the lifeless body of Jesus after He was taken down from the cross.

I remembered the words "Pietà, meaning *pity*." Only this time, I didn't feel pity; this time it was real, and it was Christ holding me! The light that surrounded us was mystical, loving and comforting. The light was bright, but it was gentle and serene to my eyes as I watched myself in Christ's arms. I saw myself three-dimensionally, from all directions, and it seemed unfamiliar and weird. I could mostly recall how I was feeling when I was with Him. It was an overwhelming, full sense of belonging; I felt so whole, so happy, so healed, so safe and so unconditionally loved. It was there that knowledge was transcended without a single word of conversation.

I remember the feeling of wanting to stay there and never leaving Jesus to come back to my life here, ever again. I knew if He asked me to come and be with Him, I would have left this world forever without the slightest hesitation.

I remember slowly lying back down into my pillow and asking myself, "What . . . *what* was that?" Did I die for a few seconds? Did I have an out-of-body experience?

There were so many mixed emotions starting to run through my blood. The one thing I did know, for sure, was that I'd been willing not to return to my loving husband and beautiful children, who were still young and needing their mother. How could that be? I loved them all so much, and normally nothing would matter more to me than to be with them.

In fact, "our famous special words" for each other, even to this day, have always been "I love you more." More to us meant, deeper than the deep blue ocean, bigger than the big blue sky, more than even my life itself! But for some reason, in this moment, I didn't value anything else, including my family or my children; I wanted to stay drinking in the beauty of Jesus and what appeared to be Heaven. It was then that I knew this was not a dream, at least not any dream I had ever experienced before. It surely had to be a Divine vision from God, and I knew, without a doubt, I would take this to my last days of my life. This must be what they consider to be "a spiritual conversion," I thought, as from this moment I knew I was forever changed. I truly felt my ordinary life was suddenly filled with purpose and meaning and I was here for a special reason with a "job to do." But what?

Strangely, the very next night, sometime shortly after I fell asleep, again I felt myself in that same familiar dark tunnel. Only this time, I saw other people and animals going through alongside of me, but at a distance. I could not make them out in detail, but I knew they were having the same experience as me.

I didn't feel the last dark emotions this time, but I could feel myself struggling and pulling myself away from the force of the light. I wasn't pulling away because it wasn't a good feeling but because it was a great feeling, and I knew it. This time, it was familiar, and I knew if I allowed myself to go there again, I would not want to return.

I struggled, with the love of my children and my other loved ones versus the purest love that I knew was waiting for me. I absolutely knew that I wouldn't want to come back, so I felt myself trying to pull away and force myself to go in the other direction; I felt like a salmon swimming upstream. In the struggle, I awoke. I lay there again, frozen with my eyes wide open, asking myself, "Why did this happen again, and more importantly, why did I stop myself this time?" The only answer I could come up with was I knew, this time, I would not want to come back, and I couldn't bear leaving my children, as they needed me here. I couldn't lose them, and they couldn't lose me. Maybe God was just giving me a second chance to make sure I wanted to remain here. When I think of this today, it brings tears to my eyes.

Over the next few days, I spent time constantly going over and over in my mind, what I had seen and felt. Normally, I could hardly remember dreams when I woke up, let alone know the reason for their existence. Yet when I became conscious and awoke from this vision—and any vision I've had since—I remembered every precise detail, and I knew their exact meaning. I wasn't sure what to make of this, but I knew "it was something" beyond a mere dream or anything I had ever felt or experienced before. I knew this was something strong and divinely special; I swore this was something I would forever remember and take to my grave, hopefully as an old woman.

Two questions were troubling me. Why did I have this vision, and what was I supposed to do with it? At the time, I felt afraid to tell anyone, as I knew everyone would discredit me or try to talk me out of the experience or, worse yet, start to think I was going crazy. People always tend to shrug off these kinds of stories and find another reason why they happened. I wanted to keep the experience sacred. Trying to explain it would dilute and diminish the incident, so I kept it to myself for a long time.

The only one I talked to about it was God himself, in my prayers, but even back then, I didn't feel I was getting a clear direction as to what I was supposed to do with this information, if anything. One day, I did finally confide in only one friend, a work colleague, during a walk. Luckily, that one friend said, "You're so lucky. I would love to have a vision."

At least one person didn't think I was going crazy, I thought, but even with that, I decided I wasn't going to do anything more because this was "mine." It was obvious I needed to put my faith to the test and commit to finding the answers for me, no matter how long it took—especially before sharing the vision with anyone else. I do remember thinking, "Why are we always willing to save someone who is experiencing a critical physical crisis, and yet we people who are having spiritual crises are afraid to tell someone something like this, especially when it could give others hope?"

After all, God is the reason for our hope.

I decided not to tell anyone else and quietly went to the library to do some of my own private research, to see if I could determine what this really was. That seemed more reasonable to me than having someone trying to talk me out of what I had just experienced. Besides, I really couldn't explain it, so how could I expect others to comprehend? After frantically scouring the Religious and Spirituality sections of the library, I remember reading parts of books on angels, reincarnation and the afterlife. Although all of these books seemed fascinating, none of them seemed to match or apply to my situation.

Then I came upon the book called *Life after Life*, by Raymond Moody, Jr., MD, Ph.D. He was, at the time, the leading authority on "near-death experiences" and the man who changed the way we viewed death and dying. At age **23**, he launched an entirely new medical field, which related to near-death studies, and began to explore the world of past lives and possible reincarnation. Then he stumbled onto the realm of visions.

His work documented reports of near-death experiences, and they seemed to mirror mine. "I'm getting closer," I remember thinking. In his work, he talked about feelings of peace, out-of-body and tunnel experiences, and being in the light—which seemed very familiar to me. Part of the joy the people experienced was the absence of everything terrible, including sin. You could feel as if everything were clean and pure perfection.

I was intrigued because, truly, until I'd had my vision, I honestly hadn't known near-death experiences existed! I had not even heard of them before. Fearful, I then started to question for a second if my heart had possibly stopped. (I did know I'd had high blood pressure since I was 19 years of age, and I was aware of all the heart disease on my father's side of the family.) Could this be possible? I whispered, "But I'm only 32 years old"—but then, so was Christ!

Since that day, for **23** years, I've kept researching and reading about this subject from authors like Melvin Morse, MD, who wrote *Closer to the Light,* and Betty J. Eadie, who wrote *Embraced by the Light.* At the same time, I kept my visions and the knowledge of them secret. Betty nearly died herself. She describes the events that followed as being "the most profound near-death experience ever." The truths she learned are worth reading and truly echo the details and emotions I discovered in my visions.

For me, apart from the research I discovered in the library, there was one confirmation in those library books on near-death experiences that deeply disturbed and consumed me. I read in these documented reports that Heaven existed outside the dimensions of both space and time and, as a result, there were reports of clocks and watches that would stop keeping time during these events.

How strange, as I had a watch that had stopped the day of my first vision.

Chapter 5
Inspirational People in My Life

(1) HERBERT

I thank my God every time I remember you.

—Philippians 1:3

My grandfather Herbert was my father's father. Born in Leith, Scotland, he immigrated to Canada as a young boy. His attestation papers for World War I stated his year of birth as 1896 because his mother gave him permission to change it from 1899 to make him eligible to join the 16th Battalion (Canadian Scottish) CEF (Canadian Expeditionary Force) in the Great War. My father was always puzzled, saying, "What kind of mother would have knowingly put her son in harm's way if she didn't have to?" It's hard to speculate on circumstances in a different lifetime.

In the trenches, shellfire landing in close proximity to my grandfather deafened him in one ear, forcing him back home from Amiens, France. Upon my visit in 2013 to the Canadian National Memorial at Vimy Ridge, I comprehended true sacrifice in colossal proportions. If only we could stop repeating the immense cost of war on all human life. I even thanked God for deafness, which challenges lives every day, including my own mother, but here at Vimy deafness appeared "simple."

Later, here in Canada, Herbert met his wife, my grand-mother Elizabeth, who served in the war as a nurse. I called her Nan, but her friends called her Bess. She was born in Falkirk, Scotland, which was a town unknown to him but not more than 50 kilometres away from his home town. They married in July 1918, which was just prior to the end of the war, and moved to the prairies with her sister and her husband to try their hand at farming. This endeavor failed, moving them back to Ontario.

My strongest recollection of my grandmother is that she read and knew the Bible like the back of her hand. These days, I'm trying to model her remarkable ability to remember Scripture. Today, I treasure the *Common Prayer Hymn Book* that my grandfather gave to her on their wedding day. I often wonder if she acquired her faith by being grateful for the blessings in her life, too.

As a young girl in 1912, Elizabeth was supposed to make a transatlantic crossing on the *Titanic,* travelling out of Southampton, England, and going to New York. She and her sister fell ill when they were given their immunization needles in preparation for the journey. Thankfully, she and her parents "missed the boat," so to speak. Sometimes we have to accept that things in life happen for a reason! There is no use wishing something had not happened, as some things you cannot change—nor would you want to if you knew the outcome. In those situations, minimizing the damage at the time and trying to learn and move forward is best, as there is no perfect family or life. Life lessons have shown me that even if you come close, you are blessed!

On a recent trip to Scotland in October 2013, I stood in the front of the house my grandmother had lived in for, yes, 13 years before immigrating to Canada. Upon visiting, I was fortunate to meet one person who is currently living in this house. When I shared with her that I was the great-grandchild of the original owner of the house, she told me how her mother and father have been researching the house, which "they believed to be over 100 years old."

"Yes," I confirmed, "the house is over 100 years old, as my grandmother lived in this house from 1899 to 1912."

She then told me something I wasn't quite prepared for. She said her family had reason to believe this house was haunted. She said, "We can hear a man's footsteps always at a certain time in the day, which would have been when he likely returned home from work. We have assumed it was the man who originally lived in this house."

While I cringed at the word *haunted,* she continued to say she had seen this unrested soul a couple of times, and she described his hat. As she did so, I remembered the photographs my father had given to me to place in the family-tree legacy books I had been preparing for my children. Strangely enough, the man in the photograph was wearing the hat as she described. Perhaps he too was born in a caul and had a Fylgiar! It made me wish my dad were still alive so I could share this story with him. My heart assures me that Dad already knows and that he is with his grandfather and my grandfather as we speak.

I was Herbert's youngest grandchild out of six. I was often told that when I was born and it was announced I was a girl, "He was thrilled."

Twenty-five years and a few days passed, and the factory retired Herbert; he came home and announced he "no longer was good for anything anymore." What he had always known as his reason to get up at every sunrise was no longer. Gazing out from under his sun hat, he realized God had given him a new purpose.

I was the new soul whom he always knew would have a special place in his heart, beyond explanation or comprehension, even to him. My hazel eyes were a pure reflection of his very own hazel eyes, and I brought so much joy and creativity to his life. As this quaint old man looked out of his back porch window, he always asked, "Have you seen Kate today?" Kate was a Scottish pet name he gave to me. His wife always warned by a quiet whisper, "Oh don't let her folks hear you call her that," but Herbert replied, "She'll always be Kate to me."

Our house was next door to my grandparents', and all the days I shared with them I remember as a special adventure. "Papa," as I called Herbert, sat in his chair listening to Mickey Mantle score a home run for his favorite baseball team, the New York Yankees. As he wore his transistor radio earphones, his eyes followed my motions as I sang and danced around him. The day before, I had taken his sun hat off his head and had made-believe I was his own personal hairdresser. According to my grandmother, this caused Herbert to somehow find great self-control and patience, because no one was allowed to even touch his hair. Not even her!

Another day, I would find some brooms from the curling arena located down the street, and I would sweep up every cigarette butt I could possibly find within a one-mile radius. The day before, I would chatter a mile a minute with him while he let me hold the garden hose as he watered the grass, which was now burned from the long hot days of the August sun. It was a ritual I cherished, even above playing with my neighbourhood mates. I figure I must have kept his mind on everything but the war, because like my neighbour Steve, Papa never talked about the war, even though I knew he had once gone there too.

How did sitting on the hot pavement, memorizing the movements of this weary old man who was making cement to mend a cracked sidewalk keep me so intrigued? What did he say to me to humour my young mind? I believe it was just the love we shared, because whatever day it was, it didn't matter. We were inseparable spirits.

All of a sudden, I would remember his eyes moving across the picket-fenced yard to Timmy. Timmy was one year older me, and he always appeared to be a whole lot larger against my petite frame. Timmy was Herbert's other friend who shared many of his retired days, lying under his chair and searching for his company and the odd pat on the head. Timmy was Herbert's dog, a cross between a Saint Bernard and Golden Lab.

Timmy also knew the special qualities I possessed; he would not tolerate anyone else doing the things that he let me do to him. He, too, trusted and was soothed by my angelic qualities, even though my footsteps were busy and often quick and unpredictable. Although I could often make him feel skittish, Timmy came to know my gentle heart was trusting, giving and loving, and quite often I held a delicious cookie, which I shared through the fence. This was likely one of my first lessons in life on trust.

* * *

Fifty more years have passed—and so, too, have both the weary old man and Timmy. In later years, my grandmother told me that amongst the crowds cheering from his ear-phones, he told her his "mind would wander." He said, "I envision Kate growing up into a fine young lady no man would ever be good enough for." He said, "I imagine her becoming a mother, a nurse or even a teacher, and I think of all the wonderful days waiting ahead of this bright, imaginative and energetic child. But today she seems to be like an angel—my angel."

The trees Herbert once said "would never give shade" now tower over the piece of the world where our special union transpired, and their house has since burned to the ground. Yet my precious memories live on in my mind and in the lives of my children through stories like these.

I've shared these stories many times, and I remember my time with my grandfather as the best summers of my life. There doesn't seem to be a day that goes by that I am not fondly reminded of the love and undivided attention that surrounded these summers. Herbert was a person who had time—made time—and slowed things down from what we now know of life. When I was at an impressionable age, he gave me a feeling of a deep and perfect love and friendship much like a friendship with Jesus.

When the roar of a diesel cement truck passes me on the road, I think of him. When I look at a dime, I think of the days he placed one in my hand to take to the dime store to buy candy. When a dog approaches me with affection and a need to be loved, I look into his eyes and think of Timmy—and Herbert.

When I watch any of the PGA Golf Tournaments and I see someone wearing a stylish straw sun hat, I get all tingly inside and smirk and think, "Herbert was before his time."

As I entered the arena at my son's hockey tournaments, the smell of the icy cold air made me immediately remember the curling brooms I used to use to sweep up his cigarette butts. I wonder what he would think of all the advancements in medicine and the decline of cigarettes. Back then, tobacco advertising was on television commercials and on billboards; they were plastered all over magazines. Now the blunt warning labels alone advertise their true value.

My warmest memories of those precious, relaxing days come to me when I hear the dull roar of cheering crowds from the stands of a ball stadium. When we travel, it is common practice for my husband and me to catch a base-ball game in the city we are visiting. I can't help but close my eyes and wish with all my might Papa was sitting in the seat right beside me, cheering.

But then again, I guess he always has been—"only for the home team!"—much like our Lord. The only real regret I have today is I can never ever remember actually telling my Papa how much I loved him. I guess it was a time when sentimental words weren't spoken as freely and as sweetly, and we had to trust our actions to display our deep feelings of love.

Later my visions told me, "So be sure to always tell people you love them because sometimes you never get another chance." Perhaps this was because there were times in the past we didn't openly talk about love.

This lesson was however learned in my early days of motherhood when I made up my mind I would never be afraid to say "I love you" to my own children. I knew I had the power to either change history or repeat it. As a result, my children would then say "I love you" to my parents, and with that small comfort level of change, it started my parents saying "I love you" back to their grandchildren. What then became really life changing was when my parents felt comfortable to say "I love you" to us! I watched the wave come full cycle and I realized I was responsible for the power of my actions that fueled and supported that positive life cycle change! Heeding this advice of my vision, I thankfully didn't make the same mistake with my own father on that last day.

I often wish that we could turn back time. My Papa Herbert was another special heart whom I would like to have a heart-to-heart chat with once again. I often wish he hadn't passed away when I was so young. Many times I have gone out to his earthly resting place, and I've had a chat with him there, but it's not like the days when I would sit on his porch with him, chatting and watering his grass.

I even placed my wedding bouquet on his grave once, as he was the one person I'd wished could have been at my wedding. Sometimes life doesn't quite work out as we would hope. Now I'm hoping he is one of those people I get to see again in Heaven. I'd like to continue our beautiful chats together. I may have lost him early on this Earthly plane, but we were never at a loss for words, and now I have so much more to tell him!

(2) ROSE

Don't look for big things; just do small things with great love.

— Mother Teresa

As I pulled into the driveway that encircled the house, I felt my baby move. This was my first-born, and I believed she was as excited as I was every time I arrived at this destination.

I talked to Rose many times a week on the telephone, but on the weekend, I couldn't wait to inhale the smell of freshly brewed coffee and feel the warmth of her welcoming kitchen.

I had come here at least a hundred times throughout my lifetime, but today I was turning 25 years old. The visit was special, but what I did not know was that it would be my last visit with this most incredible woman, a person I had admired all my life. This was the day she told me I was expecting "a girl"—a daughter.

Four days later, Rose passed away, and three months later, I experienced a miracle. My pain became my joy: my baby girl was born exactly like Rose had told me.

My grandmother's name was Rosina, and she was known as Rose. She was my mother's mother. She called me

Katerina, the Italian version of Katherine. I didn't particularly like that name, but fortunately we didn't get hung up on names. When I arrived, she only smiled and immediately made me feel loved.

She lived in a quaint, spotless, one-bedroom upstairs apartment. I remember every detail from many visits to her place when I was a young child. I used to visit there on Sunday afternoons with my parents. I called her Nona, as that is the Italian translation for *grandmother*. If I had known the Italian word for *saint*, I might have called her that, as she had the purest heart of anyone I knew.

It wasn't so much what my grandmother said that made her beautiful; it was how she treated others and how she made them feel. Her heart was kind and giving, and whatever was hers soon became yours. In fact, on that last day, she sent me home with a dozen eggs with double yolks, a tin of olive oil and a jar of homemade applesauce touched with cloves that she had just made for herself. She was so full of wisdom, but at the same time, she was polite and so humble. She wore her heart on the outside. She saw only the best in everyone and forgave and loved each and every one. She said, "We are all incredibly intuitive if we learn to become still and listen to the quiet whisper of the heart, for it knows the way."

Wisdom is one of those things that can be hard to define. If you have wisdom, are you smart? I'm sure we all know someone who may be plenty smart but who lacks wisdom.

If you have wisdom, do you have knowledge, common sense, insight or good judgment? Wisdom encompasses all of those things and more. I believe true wisdom comes from God. Being wise means being in tune with the ways of God and being in tune with the mind of God. The closer we grow to God, the wiser we become.

Rose used to tell me that His words are perfect, infallible and unfailing, always trustworthy and truthful. She used to say, "The wisdom of God is concentrated into every sentence He spoke. His words were practical, and He spoke the language of everyday people by telling simple stories."

If we could only listen to Him, we would learn how to live full, right and blessed lives—exactly like my Nona.

It was in her cozy, love-filled kitchen that I absorbed all there was to know; I became well-educated about my grandmother's beliefs and her life. Her father, my great-grandfather Innocente, who originally came from France, came to Canada from Italy to work in the Britannia Mine— which was the largest copper mine in the British Empire. This spectacular mine has now been designated a Canadian National Historic site. Over 60,000 people from 50 countries lived and worked in this isolated mining community located in British Columbia halfway between Vancouver and Whistler. It was there my great-grandfather was killed at the age of 52. He was a *trammer* and was engaged in drawing muck from a chute that was hung up. When it released with a rush it smashed through the doors, covering and suffocating this dear hardworking man. He never got the chance to return home to Italy to see his family or the house he was building with the money he sent home.

In 2011, I visited my great-grandparents' home town of Giavera del Montello in the north of Italy. One of the most moving experiences I had there was visiting the actual house where it all began, because this home was still owned and being lived in by younger generations of the family. Upon walking into the main room of this two-storey stone house, we saw a fireplace, and above the fireplace was the original large wooden framed photograph of my great-grandfather, some 80 years later! Rose's mother, Louise, my great-grandmother, raised four daughters and remained a widow living there to a ripe old age of 102, until she fell down some stairs and tumbled to her fate.

In 2015, I was fortunate to visit the Britannia Mine and was able to retrace my great-grandfather's return trip by steamship to a cemetery plot in Vancouver. What I learned: I came from a very hard-working lineage, and life for my ancestors was anything but easy!

One year before her father's death, my grandmother married my grandfather in Italy. Four years later, at the age of 30, she immigrated to Canada, bearing two children's photographs on her passport. My grandfather had already gone on ahead a couple years earlier to pave the way to immigrate to a new land.

Rose returned several times to Italy to visit her mother and her sisters. In 1978, she returned for her mother's 100th birthday celebration. In Italy, it is customary for the pope to issue Congratulatory 100th Birthday Certificates. During this time, Pope John Paul I reigned at the Vatican for a term of 33 days (August 26, 1978 to September 28, 1978). My great-grandmother's birthday was on August 27, 1978, so amazingly she is one of the very few recipients of this honourable certificate worldwide.

The last time Rose returned was after her mother's death. I remember she kept a mirror over her bedroom dresser with photographs of all her living family surrounding the outside. (Today, I have this mirror in the front hall of my home.) On the dresser below were photographs of her deceased relatives, and she would place white flowers in front of their pictures because she loved the pureness of white flowers.

Flowers, she would say, were like life itself: They blossom, they shine with perfection, and then they fade and die, just like us. People often use this symbolism to mark many milestones: births, graduations, weddings, anniversaries and funerals.

It was only later in my life that I made the connection between my grandmother and her name being a flower,

Rose. The pieces now fit together like a puzzle, but in her presence it was clouded, as I presume it was not my time to understand this little bit of harmony. As you will learn later, I use this dresser as the focal point for my prayer. I smile, as I know my family kiddingly calls it my "shrine."

Rose would do anything and give anything to anyone, regardless of what was left for herself. She often made our favourite dish, called *gnocchi*, which is nothing like anything you can buy here in stores or restaurants. When she served it, she waited on us and never sat down or ate herself. When I got older, I made her change that practice and join us. It was a habit she had brought from the old country, a habit that stayed with her from the years of the Depression. Feeding the paying boarders first and putting the hungry mouths of her children first was all she had ever known.

One thing was always perfectly clear and evident to me. She loved God and often said she was "not afraid of dying." Wonder if she herself ever had a vision. Maybe she did and never told anyone!

Nona wore a simple gold chain around her neck bearing a tiny cross, anchor and heart. These were the theological symbols for Christian faith (the cross), hope (the anchor) and charity (meaning love or generosity), and she truly did live up to these symbols in her everyday life, for generosity is all about trust. A beautiful ceramic crucifix hung over her calendar on the wall and protected her each day of her Christian life. I remember her saying, "I loved my mother and my father so much, and the happiest times in my life were when I was a child." She said, "I adored my parents, and I experienced a delightful childhood, making them the best years of my life." She now made her love for her grandchildren no secret.

My only regret is not having had the opportunity to sit down with her, and chat again after visiting the icons first-hand from her lifetime. There is never enough time! I believe, one day, I will get that chance in Heaven because, without a doubt, this woman is now one of God's angels!

Oh, and by the way, that baby I was carrying on that last faithful visit to Nona was my daughter, Jocelyne Katherine Rose, born on the **23**rd of February, 1984.

(3) ANN

Life is beauty, admire it.
Life is a dream, realize it.
Life is a challenge, meet it.
Life is a duty, complete it.
Life is a game, play it.
Life is a promise, fulfill it.
Life is sorrow, overcome it.
Life is a song, sing it.
Life is a struggle, accept it.
Life is a tragedy, confront it.
Life is an adventure, dare it.
Life is luck, make it.
Life is life, fight for it.

— Unknown

When she grew older, my mother, Ann, had the delight of her eyes taken away, and she was forced to learn her greatest lessons in this life. She reminded me of a monarch butterfly that seemed to come out of its chrysalis, time and time again, appearing in a new form. I've been truly inspired by my mother's strength and bravery, and I'm so proud of her. What I find remarkable is that in a purely uncalculated fashion, my parents once had two monarch butterflies on the front of their home!

In 1930, Ann made her voyage to North America with her mother Rose and her older sister Maria (Mary) on the

Augustus. At only two years old, she was leaving behind a country she would never remember in the same way again. As water gushed up over the portholes and the life boats were released in a violent ocean storm that almost sank the boat, even her mother began to have doubts about moving to the New World and whether it still was a good idea. The only thing my mother could remember was finally seeing Lady Liberty on Bedloe Island (Liberty Island since 1956) as they arrived. Those were the days when immigrants truly integrated into society and later made up the greater population of the new America.

In 1937, during the Great Depression, the family moved to northern Ontario so her father could work in the gold mines, because that was where work was available. These Depression years were harsh, and not just because of the climate.

Boarders lived at my grandparents' home, which helped supplement the family income. They raised their own chickens, had outdoor gardens in the good weather, and had gardens in the basement to grow and raise their own food in the winter.

My mother recalls the horrors of her mother asking her as a young child to go and get a chicken for dinner. "Bring me back a chicken who hasn't laid an egg," her mother told her. As my mother loved all animals, she would return saying, "They all had eggs," which would only get her further into trouble.

My mother recalls Nona using soap mixed with bleach to scrub their wood floors; they didn't have much, but at least everything they did have was spotlessly clean. They had an outside bathroom until her father built an add-on bathroom with a toilet and sink at the back of the house. Mary and Ann would walk down the railroad tracks at lunchtime to deliver boxed lunches to their father and the boarders, who were working at the nearby mines. My grandfather hated working in the mines after what had happened to his father-in-law so they also gave him cement work to do which was the trade he brought with him from Italy. Along the way from the mines, the girls would pick wild blueberries. Rattlesnakes had a habit of lying on the tracks to bask in the hot summer sun. Whenever this happened, the girls were startled and dropped the baskets, and the berries never made it home.

Their family soon grew by one son and two more daughters; however, the last baby girl lived only ten minutes after delivery—they had just enough time to call a priest to baptize her before she died. Years later, I learned this baby, who was named after her grandmother, Louise, was born almost 40 years to the day before my baby girl. Today, an angel stands over Louise's gravesite.

Not long after that family tragedy, my mother met my father on a hayride for which they had arrived separately, with blind dates. My father described it as "love at first sight"; he knew instantly he wanted to marry and spend his entire life with my mother. In a letter that he wrote in his 78th year, which we found after Dad's passing, he described this time by saying, "I wish I could spend another lifetime together with you."

Now, as I stare at my mother, I see she wears Dad's wedding ring on the same gold chain around her neck along with her gold cross. I listen to her stories about being married 65 years, 9 months and 7 days. She was only a child of 18 when she said, "I do."

She has taken a long journey in time to get to this place, even though the years meld into what now seems like only moments. The man she absolutely loved and lived for each day has now vanished.

As she hears the elevator door open to their fourth-floor apartment, she tells me she still expects to see him come through the door, smiling and carrying his library books.

And then she stares at me and says, "But I know he won't be coming through that door ever again, no matter how hard I wish." She clings to the knowledge that her religion has given her a set of beliefs she has held ever since she was a young girl.

Her husband is now gone to live in a Heaven, which she has believed in for as long as she can remember. Today, somehow, all that doesn't seem much consolation; it hardly fills the void that is left in her heart. Her memories fill her brain, but her heart is left empty. The only tangible proof of life, and love, is her wedding ring on her hand and Dad's gold wedding band, which swings from the gold chain around her neck.

Each night, she stares at their wedding photograph, which has always been displayed in the centre of their dresser in their bedroom. She sees the young pretty woman she once was standing beside the young handsome man with whom she shared nearly her whole life. As she kneels down in prayer, she whispers, every night, to the photograph, and then she retires to the lonely bed. "Why did you have to leave me?" she whispers. With tearful eyes she says, "I wish we could start over and do it all again. I love you, and I miss you *so* much."

I recall a deep conversation I had with my mother on December **13**, 2014. It was at a moment that she, once again, became an important part of my life after a very long time. I felt I was truly and finally "with my mother" by helping her heal her sorrow and pain while recalling her joyous life memories.

My brother always said to me, "You are the epitome of empathy," adding that he believed that my health had failed because of my weakness of caring too deeply and selflessly for people. It may be a curse, but it could also be strength when you have empathy! Having the intuitive ability to interpret the emotions of others is a very powerful gift. But my brother was right when he said it also makes it easier to take on too much negativity and anxiety. Learning how to harness this emotion for the good, to become a proactive humanitarian, is the key, but this has been a lifetime struggle for me.

During the conversation, my mother described how she and my father had met. Her facial expressions changed from smiles to frowns as she remembered Dad giving her an engagement ring and then leaving home under duress. She recalled how they didn't have two pennies to rub together, yet they knew they had each other and that love would sustain them. And it did!

She described her life as an immigrant, through the Depression and being on "relief," as she called it. It was the first time I understood what "doing without" and "making do" meant. I finally understood how that experience made her the way she was today. I saw my mother in a much different light than I remembered from my childhood days, and I appreciated how and why my life was different from hers. Later, the same evening, I found myself awakened from sleep, crying. Through those tears, I also found myself thanking God for this special time and insight and for bringing me closer to my mother than I had ever been in 56 years. Sometimes our eyes need to be washed by our tears so we can see in front of us with a clearer vision.

Although my father named me, one of my mother's favourite stories is why she "cried to be a mother." I find the story of *my beginning* as interesting as my father's birth.

Our mother underwent two fertility surgeries that were performed by Dr. Earl Plunkett, Chief of Gynecology at London's University Hospital before she was able to conceive her two children. Dr. Plunkett was an internationally respected physician, fertility authority and teacher. He was one of a select group of international experts, brought together to approve the new concept of endocrine suppression of ovulation by a hormone found in a plant. This led to the development of the first birth control pill and research into in vitro fertilization.

Later, he worked with renowned neurosurgeon Dr. Charles Drake, researching the surgical and endocrine control of hormonally active cancers such as in the breast and prostate. Their work together helped produce major breakthroughs in the field of endocrinology. I find it amazing that this same physician not only helped bring me into the world but also helped keep me here through cancer research!

In fact, when we were children and we were misbehaving, Mom would say those words more directly: "And to think I cried to be a mother!" I pray she forgives me for all the mistakes I've made as a daughter. Now, since my dad has passed, my mother tells me she loves me every day I talk to her, and we tell each other how much we love each other. It brings me great joy as I look at her and I say, "This is why you cried to be a mother," and then I add, "Mom, you are not alone now, and Dad is still here with you through us."

One sunny, cold winter day, I had my mother in the car with me as I stopped to donate some items to a shelter for battered women. On the way back, I knew I was close, so I took a detour and drove down some familiar streets I knew Mom would quickly recognize, as her mind is still sharp.

Things had changed. I watched her face as we drove by the original neighbourhood and down the street where Dad and Mom had their first home together. We started chatting and recalled what had changed and what was still there. The garage seemed smaller, but the tree Dad had planted in the backyard behind it was overwhelmingly huge. I stared at the kitchen window, remembering the day I could have been killed. It was fun to share and recall the past together. It was like looking at the same original window painting we both knew at one time.

Still, it was painful for both of us, remembering how much my mother and father put into that home and realizing that all the neighbours were now gone. We both realized how much time had passed and how time never stands still for anyone. She told me about three houses in town that had been built by her father, Bruno, and she showed me where my father's parents had lived before moving to the house I knew as theirs.

Learning family history is a wonderful gift; you just have to put down your current toys and actually make time before time runs out! It was a remarkable discovery for me, and I also got to enjoy a great lunch with my mother.

By the second year after the passing of my father, everyone in their age group seemed to be leaving this earthly plane: first my Dad's closest cousin, then my mother's cousin's husband, then a friend at their church. The death of a girlfriend of my mother, whom she had known for years, followed. She had been Mom's maid of honour when my parents married. These sad occasions continued within such a short time frame. Next it was a dear and close friend of my mother, and after that, another close friend of my dad. Then it was a neighbour who lived across the street for 40 years.

Looking at the complete picture now, it's like my dad was voted off the island first, like the people on some of those reality shows on television. All I could think about was my dad being first; maybe he was given the job of being the welcoming committee in Heaven. Maybe it's for the best; my dad would have been hurt deeply if he were still here and would spend even more time obsessing about his own mortality. Instead, he gets to welcome family and friends with his big, beautiful, inviting smile!

Losing sight of eternity cannot be confused with losing the sight of God. My mother never lost sight of God her whole life; she continually prayed and attended Mass for as long as I can remember, and she still does. Often, they call her "the oldest altar server"! In fact, I owe my spiritual focus to my mother; she has been a catalyst and a constant guiding light.

Up until my dad's passing, Ann lived in pretty much an imaginary world. Some days, I wondered if it were "her creative way" of coping with all the obstacles and changes in her life. Some people might say she was "just being in denial," but I've learned denial is a strong survival mechanism. I realized it was about helping her accept each day with grace.

Right from the start, Ann chose not to confront the seriousness of my dad's heart condition; it wasn't that the doctors or the family never tried to explain it to her. She basically took his illness at face value and never imagined the truth about what was going on in the inside. She also never imagined—or allowed herself to think about—Dad dying someday and leaving her here.

She would say, "I really thought we would grow old together." Under my breath, I would say, "You did!" They were in their mid-80s, and they had been married 67 years minus two months! When my father died, it was like my mother was waking up from a 67-year sleep, at which time she started to return to her more independent days. Heartbreakingly chronic pain and physical limitations started to diminish her determination and increase her loneliness. A small heart attack this summer awakened her awareness even more.

Watching her reaction to the announcement of the birth of her first great-grandchild after she had been widowed was both joyous and painful. Her great granddaughter, Isabelle, arrived on June 16, 2015 (6 + 1 + 6 = **13**) at 6:43

a.m. $(6 + 4 + 3 = \mathbf{13})$ Australia time, and the numbers were no surprise to me. Isabelle was six months old when mom finally got to embrace her (and wouldn't put her down!) She presented a very special gift to her—a gold chain containing the same faith, hope and charity symbols not unlike the one her own mother wore. What a lucky little girl—the baton will have been passed to yet another generation.

After watching health issues arise, we become more attuned to each new sunrise, which brings along with it newly awakened lessons learned in the ocean of our souls. As each wave touches us, we learn, right to our very last breath, and the ripple of each wave touches the rest of us. It is hard to watch the people whom we love dearly get sick; suffer loneliness, pain and loss; and eventually fade and die like the flowers.

Why is it that we tend to have such a narrow view of life? It's always been part of the human condition, yet I think it has become more prevalent of late. The "me generation" continues to bloom, yet we seem to become more short sighted, and it appears we have lost sight of eternity.

In the Bible, Jesus encourages us to take the long view. Those who take this brief time on Earth for granted and use it to satisfy the rewards of the flesh risk losing their eternal reward. I understand this concept because I'm married to an investment advisor; I compare life to investing. My husband has always told me to take the long view in investing. He says the market is volatile, but if you invest wisely, the highs and the lows will level out and you will achieve your goals.

It's best to start early, just as it is best to start early in determining your spiritual path. So waste no time, and start asking God to give you the grace to conduct your life as though your eternity depended on it; start planning today for your retirement from this world.

One of the dearest gifts I received from my mother came from a third party. It was through a friend who had called my mother to see how she was doing. My mother told my friend how she sees me. In Mom's words, "I think Kate is a lot like my mother. My mother, Rose, was such a lovely woman, and I see Kate has those same qualities. She also is a good friend, so it is no wonder she has lots of good friends herself."

Mom continued to say how loyal I was and how that is a wonderful quality in a friendship. She told my friend three times how special I was to her. She said I was a wonderful person, not because of what I do but because of who I have become. Mom ended the conversation by saying that I do so much for her, as do my brother and his wife. "I have a really good family," Mom said.

If only my mother could see all the things she is still teaching us. I'm so glad God sent me to my mom, to be my mother. I have been *so* blessed in this lifetime.

I treasure every second God allows Mom to remain here with us. Like all my friends who have lost their parents say, "You never look forward to becoming an orphan."

Chapter 6
Early Visions

What do you think? If a man owns a hundred sheep, and one of them wanders away, will he not leave the ninety-nine on the hills and go to look for the one that wandered off? And if he finds it, I tell you the truth, he is happier about that one sheep than about the ninety-nine that did not wander off.

—Matthew 18:12–13

God is always looking after us when we go astray—no matter how far we go or where we are. And when we hear His voice and return, there is much rejoicing.

—Gus Lloyd

I like to think of my life as being guided not by fate but rather by freedom of choice and the consequences that follow those free-will decisions. I have learned that any sizable decision has the potential to significantly change lives. We often see this more clearly looking back, but then hindsight, as they say, is always 20/20 vision. It's funny how when we meet the fork in the road and we have to make a choice that choice can change the outcome of our lives totally. Looking back, we can always wonder what would have happened if we had taken the other road.

Fate, for me, was the day my mother and my friend's mother met in the beauty salon. Both of us were in our mothers' wombs, and unbeknownst to us, we would become lifelong friends. "Sisters by choice," we often later called ourselves. The beginning of our friendship reminds me of the story of Mary being pregnant with Jesus at the same time as her cousin, Elizabeth, was pregnant with John the Baptist. Even in the womb, the Bible says, John the Baptist leapt with excitement about the coming of his cousin. John knew his mission was to humbly point the way to Jesus, seeking no glory for himself, regardless of the consequences. He wanted only to glorify the One who was worthy of glory and praise.

My friend and I were officially introduced when we met in kindergarten. She made her first star turn after she noticed her mother had left. She reacted by escaping the classroom and running back towards home. I never knew teachers could run so fast. As for me, I was too busy playing with all the toys in my new surroundings to notice all the chaos she created that first day of school.

By the second day, we had become friends. It seems like no time at all, but that day turned into years, right before our eyes. We started out as young playmates, playing dress-up with our dolls. We started escorting each other to the library, and then we teamed up for school assignments. We spent a lot of time at each other's homes, swimming in my pool, celebrating our birthdays with our mutual friends and comparing notes on our brothers—we each had one.

By secondary school, we started to make birthdays miserable for each other as we decorated and taped each other's lockers with wads of masking tape in between classes. At lunch, all was forgiven, and we presented each other with a birthday cake. Ours was a forgiving kind of love; we knew this friendship was indeed special.

As the years passed, we came to that fork in the road, and both of us trailed off on our own journeys. Although our lives and our responsibilities became different from each other's, we still kept in touch and continued to do sporadic things for each other. She performed so many creative acts of kindness for my children when they were small, and I dropped things off at her house to brighten her day at a time when she was buried deep in the caretaking for her father.

That was when I had the next vision.

It was a dark room, and everyone was dressed in black. It felt like it had been pouring rain in this room. I couldn't see anyone's faces, but the smell of grief and sadness was more than I could stand. Everyone I approached covered their faces and turned away. I started to panic, as I wanted to see whose funeral this was. Suddenly, I realized it was hers. How could this be?

My eyes opened wide. I was cold and shaking, yet I felt the message was clear, and I felt concerned.

For days, I could not get this scene out of my head, and I felt part of two worlds. For days, I contemplated whether I should telephone her and tell her. What would I say? "Hello, how are you? It's me. I don't know how to tell you this, but I just attended your funeral, and it was dreadful"? How could I say that? It scared me to think of telling someone that, but then again, because it seemed so real, it also scared me *not* to tell her. I pondered, "What do I do?"

It took several days of soul-searching, but I finally made the right decision. I decided that I had to tell her. It was a difficult story to work into a cheery conversation. The only thing I had going for me was years of trusted endearment. I felt quite like a dark angel bearing tidings of sad news.

When I finally found the words, there was silence on the other end of the receiver. It made me feel worse.

I sputtered and said, "Don't worry about this or anything. It's likely nothing, but I hope you understand why I felt compelled to tell you at least."

It was then that I realized she wasn't aware of my first vision. Just as well, I thought. At least I felt better, like this huge weight had been lifted off my shoulders. Afterwards, I felt like I truly had dropped a bomb. But at the time, we simply talked briefly; she didn't let on that the grenade had bothered her in the slightest, I remembered rationalizing. Whew!

Three months passed, and then the telephone rang. It was her. She quietly thanked me for telephoning her three months ago and proceeded to tell me that she had been going through a rough time when I called. "You saved my life, Kate," she said. "After you told me about my funeral, it was your phone call that prompted me to sign myself into the hospital on the Psychiatric ward. I needed some help. I was actually contemplating suicide."

You could have heard a pin drop. To this day, I'm not sure what my response was, but I know I've never forgotten how significant this vision became.

Many times later, we talked about it, and I forever thank God for giving me the courage, common sense and conviction to recognize His signs. I also thank God for His healing and how He has changed her life.

Life, as we know it, is never perfect, but I've tried to be more aware of the problems of others, and I've tried to make myself available to helping them. In our culture, it is so easy to move along in our own lives, but we really need to engage and invest in caring about others; we need to walk with them. You should try it sometime, because I find that by helping others, the return back to me is tenfold. It always makes me feel like I've healed myself in the process.

Some people may say this was a coincidence, but I've learned that when you are open to God's work, sometimes you need to stop and connect the dots, to take the time to genuinely value someone who needs you. You can't always see clearly at the time; what appears to you to be an insignificant random act of kindness can turn out to be a life-changing moment for someone else.

I once heard a deacon speaking about how he spent some time in South America while he was a training to become a professional soccer player. He was earning high recognition for his sporting abilities, and a mayor or some dignitary presented him with a cheque to support him. This deacon donated the award money to buy sporting equipment for the underprivileged. (He had noticed that they were making soccer balls out of anything they could find and roll up.)

When asked how we, as individuals, can make a difference daily in our lives, he explained that we all don't have to give away or send monetary gifts. Everyone has special and unique God-given gifts. We all just need to be creative and use those God-given gifts to help others. By doing so, we are also better able to lead others to Christ. Are you using your gifts to accomplish this mission Jesus has given you? Sometimes it takes a long time to understand that everything is a gift, freely given from God, and it is more blessed to give than to receive. Generosity is always the greatest when it seeks nothing in return.

In the Gospel, Matthew 6 reminds us that Jesus tells us to "store up treasures in Heaven. For where your treasure is, there also will your heart be."

I believe that each time we perform an act of kindness for another person or put aside our own selfish desires and put someone before ourselves, we store up treasures in Heaven. If our treasure is spent only on the material things in the world, that's where our hearts will stay. But when we channel our treasure into the gifts from Heaven (love, kindness, service), our hearts will soar Heavenward. On my final day, as I stand before our Maker, I hope He is proud of me. I hope I have made good of the "second chance" He gave me "after cancer." I am but a simple soul who dedicated my life to changing others by sharing "my treasures." **Twenty-three** years of Divine messages took me **23** months to document. At least I can say, "I tried my best!"

Shortly after my father passed away, I took my elderly mother to the grocery store. I had to step away for a short time and leave my mother, who now weighs 100 pounds soaking wet. My mother started to struggle with the grocery carts that were held together by a chain; a quarter was required to release one. A kind soul came to her rescue and helped her release her grocery cart. It cost only a few moments of his time, but my mother turned to me and said, "You know there are more good people in this world than not. That man was so kind to come and help me." Her optimistic attitude allowed her to see the best in people and believe that all people are born with goodness inside their hearts and that through compassion, communication and understanding the world can be a better place.

In this world, you never know what your kind deeds can change. You never know what other people might be going through. In this case, my mother had just lost her best friend of 67 years, who used to help her do these simple things in life. Life just became a struggle.

You didn't know that, but you made a difference in someone else's life in the three minutes that you chose to go out of your way to help someone else! You just stored up a treasure in Heaven. Ordinary people can change the world just like a fireman can by risking his life for a perfect stranger. Be generous and cheerful—it doesn't always have to be monetary things. Giving of yourself costs nothing.

Thank you, kind stranger, for working God's magic through you. Pass it on and repeat your small favours.

Why are we too often shy, scared or too busy to help others? Find it in your heart to make others smile. Do you not think this could be God calling out to us to complete some kind of unique task? How do you know God has not used someone else as His messenger? When we are given the opportunity to become a humble servant, we grow in love. We become more compassionate. And in that way, we live in peace. We receive blessing after blessing just by performing one random act of kindness—time and again. That's how you change the world!

I'm reminded of the time a man and his wife came up to my husband and me at the airport. He asked us if we would like a deli sandwich that they had bought but hadn't touched. They had bought two sandwiches, but because the sandwiches were larger than they had anticipated, they could not eat both. Little did they know that we had become ill on the last two days of our vacation and we were anxiously trying to get home. During the last two days of our holiday, we had both eaten sparingly and had become too weak and fatigued to want to stand in line for anything let alone food. The man came over just as I was about to pass out on the dirty airport carpet. My husband offered to buy the man and his wife a coffee for their act of kindness, but he graciously refused.

I'll always remember what he said: "Thanks for the thought, but *pay it forward*. I have five children of my own. I'd really like to think maybe someone will do something good for one of them someday in return."

Yes, this also works in return. Have you ever really needed a hand from someone, but it was very difficult to ask for and accept help of others? The next time someone offers us help, instead of letting your pride get in the way, see the hand of God providing for us through the kindness and generosity of others.

A simple act of caring can create an endless ripple that comes back to you. Maybe you think you know who God will use to speak to you. But maybe God has a different plan.

Remember, we can never *out give* God. God gave us His everything—even His own precious Son.

Chapter 7
My Gifts

Yesterday is the past, tomorrow is the future, but today is a gift. That's why it's called the present.

— Bill Keane

A *gift* is defined as something voluntarily given, without payment in return, to show favour toward someone, to honour an occasion or to make a gesture of assistance. A gift is often presented wrapped in attractive paper and decorated in ribbons and bows.

Even though our entire lives are precious gifts—the pleasure, the pain—it's all part of our path. Then there are the other great gifts. These are the kind of gifts given to us throughout our lifetimes; they are known as God-given gifts and talents. These are not wrapped in pretty paper and bows, but they all are unique and different spiritual gifts given to us all by the Holy Spirit.

Sometimes, you can't see the gifts others have because you can't see past their faults. If your own giftedness is unrecognizable to you, I suggest praying about it and asking that it be revealed to you. Your special gift usually has something to do with what you love.

Giving is the secret to receiving. Share your gifts freely, and you will be surprised at how much beauty in life flows back to you.

The Bible says the gifts God has given you and the call He has put on your life are "irrevocable," which means He will never take them back. It is up to you to make the best of these gifts and to answer His call. Gifts come with strings attached. If God has been generous to us and we hoard or accumulate or squander those blessings, there will be a price to pay.

Spiritual gifts are gifts that God uses, according to His purpose, for the building of the Church. Being a spiritually sensitive person, I know it is important to walk close to God, know His word (the Bible) and adhere to His commandments. Jesus came here to fulfill the Scriptures, not to abolish them. We do not need to seek the answers from the Godly world through the use of psychics or mediums. I don't claim to be any of these. I claim only to seek God's kingdom and righteousness.

The first gifts I was given in life were my parents. My parents' love and ability to teach us the life lessons was truly a blessing from God. It isn't until later in life that we sometimes realize how fortunate we have been. As I said in my father's eulogy, "The happiest people don't always have the best of everything; they just make the most of everything they have."

Sometimes, possessions and riches can actually be corrosive and can put up obstacles as much as they can open doors. For us, we were rich in love and generous; we were people who put their trust in God.

I've heard some people say we pick our parents before we come to this world. Isn't that an interesting concept! If this is the case, then when I look around, I know I have picked well. But perhaps it was really God's plan all along.

My mother and I were going through a book of important papers, and she discovered two letters, written by Dad and sealed and addressed to me and my brother. "Open this when I am gone" were the words he had scrawled on the envelopes. My mother didn't know Dad had written these letters; it also seemed strange that they appeared to us **13** days into our grief.

Dad had written these letters after he discovered he had several life-threatening things wrong with him. He felt he should put down some of his thoughts and memories he cherished and carried around in his mind and heart. In my letter, he admitted he should have sat down with me, one-on-one, and told me about his memories, but he said life is busy, and sometimes we never make the time for the really important things. The first part of his letter contained his recollections and memories—the ones he held closest to his heart—right from the time my parents were expecting me to my days as an adult.

He told me how much they had really wanted me, a second child; my life would complete his million-dollar family, as they already had been blessed with a son. He said that I was "no accident." They had been having trouble having children, and fortunately, they had found a doctor who was able to help them conceive both my brother and me after being childless for eight years. (I was born over 11 years into their marriage.)

Dad said I brought them much happiness, even before I was born, and they looked forward—in anticipation—each day my mother carried me. Dad said, "Yes, even that long ago, I said my prayers, and as I prayed, I hoped you would be a girl so you could complete our family."

His greatest joy was watching us grow, and he loved birthdays and the Christmas season. He told me how he lost his job two months after I was born, a month after Christmas. He took a job earning $1.30 an hour and never worked so hard in all his life. He stayed at that job for a year and then started looking somewhere else.

He found a new job which didn't pay much better—$1.35 an hour—but it would one day provide a pension, and it was closer to home. Because they were having a tough time and couldn't seem to get ahead, my mother decided to get a job to help with the financial situation. Because he worked the night shift, he babysat us while my mother worked days. He said he would get us up in the morning, get us both breakfast and make sure my brother got off to school. Then he would get me washed and dressed, and then we would make the beds together.

He said, "It didn't take you long to learn the song *I Had a Dream, Dear,* as we used to sing it every day."

I would then play with my dolls; he would catnap on the couch if I left him alone.

"You always had something to ask me and would come and pat me on the cheek to wake me up," he said.

In the letter, Dad admitted that we were very close, and it brings tears to my eyes over 50 years later to know he felt what I also have felt.

He described my brother then coming home for lunch and how he would try to make sure, when he dished up the soup, that we would take turns winning the contest of who had the most lima beans in their bowl. Dad said, "I never got to win."

After lunch, he put me down for a sleep, and later he prepared the vegetables my mother wanted for supper. When she came home, we would all eat together. He went to bed right after supper because he had to work all night.

He said I was truly the first vegetarian, as I would hide my meat under my bed when they left the table to go outside to sit with their tea. Later, our Beagle, Rebel, became my friend and learned to sit under the table so I could pass my unwanted meat to him.

Dad reminded me how my mother was all business, but he always found the time to blow bubbles at bath time and participate in all the simple games we played and go to the places we went together—now that's *love.*

School was never easy for me, and Dad took responsibility for this. "Maybe it's partly our fault," he said. "We never realized you needed to wear glasses at a young age."

We sat many nights at the kitchen table doing spelling and the multiplication tables, but he said "You always worked hard", and he commented on how I did well in high school. He said "You were pretty easy to raise. You were well liked, and as a young girl, you took on responsibility and you worked hard. You have been trustworthy all your life."

"Nothing beats you," he said. "You finish what you start."

He often wondered if he hurt my feelings when he used to say, "Someday you will be beautiful." But he knew he would find the right day to tell me I was beautiful—on my wedding day. He told me right before he walked me down the aisle. In hindsight, I know he planned that!

Later, he realized that I had gone through a lot for a young woman: a marriage breakup, having to sell my house, working and being a single parent with a small child. But he said I was a determined woman and usually accomplished what I set out to do and got what I wanted. He said how proud he always was of me and my brother and how they always tried to be there for us, as he knew someday he wouldn't be. But he had confidence because of the way we turned out. "You'll do great," he said. "You have great kids, so give them all the love you can because they are adults far too soon."

The last two pages were written and added four years later, when I was undergoing my chemotherapy treatments. What he said was the purest example of unconditional love possible: "Mom and I really feel sorry about what you are going through with this disease. I wish it was me instead of you. I have had a good life, so it wouldn't matter. If it was possible, I would do it in a minute."

"I am thankful you have a good husband who has been there for you during your fight. I just pray everything works out for you."

What another gift it was, finding these letters.

A week later, in a book of business papers, we found yet another letter entitled "My Feelings and Advice." In this letter, he told us how important it is to see each other and get our families together once in a while and to forgive each other for our faults. He told us how proud he was and that he hoped we also had good memories.

He encouraged us to let our children know how much we loved them and to help them as much as we could. "Life can be hard sometimes," he said, "and they need to have someone they can count on during these times."

Dad was a great reader, and he left me with something he had read. It stuck in his mind: "Without a good woman, there would be no meaning for living today. Without children, there would be no reason to live for tomorrow. For we live on by being a small part of these, our children and grandchildren. And with this thought, death holds no fears."

Today, I deeply cherish the undivided time I can spend with my mother. Sickness and death has taught me to treat every day as a gift, as the loss of my father was unmeasurable.

Instead of asking God why, or how come, allow the valleys in your life to teach you the reasons. Those who are touched by the presence of God in this life will truly live with the hope of the fullness of God's presence in the life to come. All Christians are sent into the world to communicate this reality in whatever way they are gifted.

Think about joy versus happiness. Happiness is worldly, and joy is God-given. God-given joy comes from the peace

He gives us. My first vision was a lesson about the incredible peace He gives us, and the letters I was given by my father, although they hurt my heart still, were a true blessing from God to provide me with God's peace through dad. Happiness can be fleeting and superficial.

Sometimes, it may feel impossible to feel happiness in times of great distress, trial or struggles. These are the times that try our very souls, as we have seen with many of the great spiritual masters down through the ages. One way to start is by thanking God for His daily gifts, like a sunrise or sunset; the new voices of spring after a long, cold winter when the birds return; a card, a note or a meal that arrives unexpectedly from a thoughtful friend; the sound of much-needed pouring rain and the fragrance of flowers in the breeze; the tears brought on by memories of holding your babies; and hugs from your loved ones no longer with you.

It doesn't mean being in a good mood most of the time or experiencing the emotion of joy. Happiness is a way of life, an overriding outlook forged by qualities such as optimism, bravery, love and fulfillment.

Often, it is only when the storms arrive that we look to God. But if life weren't hard, how would we know what we are made of, and how would we really learn without comparison? When you have joy, it comes from deep within the heart. When we have complete trust and confidence, it comes from God, and God provides you peace. True joy goes much deeper than happiness, and it provides an inner quality of healing and uplifting when you are connected to God.

One day, I ran into a person who had given me what seemed to be a small, insignificant gift many, many years ago. It was a candle in a small glass dish, surrounded by white berries. It wasn't until recently that I started using this candle, in front of pictures of those I've lost. I came to realize, many years after the fact that I should tell her how special her gift turned out to be for me.

God's love can have a wave effect. People can touch your life without even knowing it. That's why I think it is so important to tell people how they have affected your life by their gestures, no matter how small or how long ago. We often even neglect to thank those closest to us. We take them for granted. A gesture of gratitude might be unexpected, but it will never go unappreciated. Go ahead and change someone's life!

My mother painted the most remarkable paintings with oil and watercolour paints. I always loved and looked forward to receiving Mom's watercolour-painted Christmas cards, and I saved every one of them. My father's woodworking and poetry took first place.

It was obvious I inherited my creative and passionate artistic talent from my parents, but I recognized my other God-given gift—my vision. (Now, I'm not saying I have a perfect 20/20 Earthly vision, because I don't. I've worn glasses or contacts from the time I was 10 years old!) I say this because I've always been a visual person. Everything has been presented to me through visions and visuals, never by way of voices.

A dear friend's father, who was undergoing chemotherapy at the same time as me, once remarked he received an audible call from God. He heard a voice in the middle of the night, during a time of great distress and chaos. It said, "All your fears will be removed."

I believe God speaks to us constantly, and it is only when we are listening that we become open to hearing God. This dear man's age, and the unkind side effects, made it impossible to complete his chemotherapy treatments. But since hearing "that voice," which his heart was open to receiving, he has been diagnosed as "cancer-free." Four years after this incident, I finally met this delightful man personally.

We had shared some words in cards and some small inspirational gifts during our darkest hours, but when I met him, he handed me 12 beautiful red roses!

There are so many different ways that God can speak to us. More commonly, He uses the Liturgy and the Scriptures, but sometimes we'll hear Him speak to us through a song or maybe through the voice of another person. For example, Elijah experienced a mighty wind, earthquake and fire, but none of these contained the audible voice of God. Elijah actually heard it in the stillness.

To do this today, try to block out all the media noise fighting for your attention, and pay closer attention at a deeper level for spiritual signs. For it is in the silent moments of life, when we still our own hearts and minds, that we are able to hear God most clearly. I somehow don't think it is a coincidence that in the English language, *listen* and *silent* contain the same block of letters. Are you making time for stillness and solitude in your life?

Dragonflies have eyes that can cover a full 360 degrees of vision. Did you know that even with our peripheral vision, humans can cover only half that range? At best, at any given moment in life, we humans are missing half of what is going on around us. Only too often, ours is a limited perspective, and this applies to us spiritually, too. Because we aren't spiritually attuned, we don't see things from God's perspective.

For me, one of the greatest miracles happened through His grace on my daughter's 30th birthday. I had redesigned my original engagement ring from my first marriage to give to my daughter on her special birthday. After this beautiful exchange, my daughter's stepmother shared with her that, even though she was the third party involved in my first marriage's breakdown, she felt it was I who carried the cross for her.

At the time my marriage fell apart, she had recently lost her husband in a sudden and tragic tractor-trailer accident. The trauma of the accident had also caused her to lose her unborn child. She now admitted to my daughter that she had always felt that I was the one who had carried the pain of her grief, because I lost my marriage for her happiness. I could never explain it, but for 30 years, I always felt this woman was a guardian angel for my daughter, to protect her from terrible alcoholic circumstances, but I never imagined seeing this side of God's plan in such depth.

Sometimes, moral obstacles prevent us from seeing the whole picture, and sometimes we don't view them as stepping stones but only perceive them as roadblocks. With her confession, it was like she had given me a looking glass, a lens of clarity, from which I could see why our lives entwined and how all our lives have a complex purpose and meaning in God's grand and mystical design.

This sincerely taught me how a shift in tone can make us learn how to love unconditionally and how to forgive and survive our wounds. How do we know if we can see clearly? It is when we stop judging another soul who possesses a different set of insights or principles than our own.

During the writing of this book, another miracle was shown to me. I had arranged to meet a friend to accompany her to the cemetery of a mutual co-worker who had suddenly passed away with cancer. I was out of the country at the time, but we both felt we really hadn't had the opportunity to properly say goodbye. On this one particular warm summer evening, we sat on the cemetery grass beside her plot, talking about the old times and very special moments the three of us had shared together.

Right or wrong, we opened a bottle of simple fruit wine and toasted our friend. We could practically feel our departed friend smiling down upon us. She would have loved it. As the sun lowered in the sky that evening, our conversation changed, and we began to talk about our lives. My friend had recently suffered the unbearable loss of triplet grandchildren, and consequently, the subject of my book came up. I let my guard down and shared some of my most intimate spiritual experiences with her in that "quiet time." It was a beautiful evening that both of us described as "touching," one that "brought the final two of us closer together."

Here is the unexpected and joyful e-mail I received from her one week later:

> "WOW! Kate, you are the best. I went to church yesterday, and couldn't stop thinking of you the entire time. The theme was the HOLY SPIRIT which is a hard concept to explain. But, I kept thinking of our chat, and that inner voice and it was explained as being the voice of the Holy Spirit. How cool is that!!!!!!!!"

In my prayers, after receiving this e-mail, God told me, "You can't change the whole world overnight, but you can start by changing one person at a time." This is what I'm hoping to do by telling my life stories.

For me, all my signs of hope have come visually, and when I think about it, so, too, have all my gifts in my life. I excelled in photography. I photographed weddings in every religion and in every location possible. This made me appreciative and open to accepting all religions. Since my cancer, by God's grace, I've reassessed my priorities and have kept my photography on a more personal level. Now I focus my time and draw my attention toward family and friends, human interest subjects, travelling, animals and nature. The world is a magical place which is filled with goodness, hope and beauty.

My other greatest gifts in my life have indeed been my children, and each child has made me a better person. Fittingly, my first child was born on February 23. Although my first marriage turned out to be a trying time in my life, my daughter Jocelyne was one of my best gifts I've ever received. I learned a lot of lessons through that marriage breakdown process, but I can't imagine for one minute my life without her bright and loving presence in my life. The moment I looked in her eyes, all my dreams became true. She made me a mother forevermore, and it's one of the most important roles upon this Earth. Although she never came with instructions, the mistakes I made came from lack of understanding, never the lack of love. And from day one, she has continued to teach me every day.

It is like a saying I once heard: "Redheads are God's way of giving the world roses." Jocelyne is indeed a redhead, and one of her middle names is Rose—after my dear grandmother!

My second marriage gave me my two stepsons, James and Kristopher. Although the second time around was not something any of us planned or wanted at the time, I hope they both know I'm so grateful and blessed that they came into and shared my life. It took me a long time to realize that it wasn't that they didn't want me; it was that they wanted their mother.

Sometimes I wondered if I was a step above or a step below; I was always feeling like an outsider, trying to fit in. It was hard, sometimes, to know their true feelings or if they were only for show. In my heart, I loved them like they were my own, and I tried to do all the things a kid's real mom would do, including consoling them when they were sad and handing out punishment if they were bad.

I felt I was there for them, even though real moms seem to get all the glory. Many times, in the early years, I hid my tears when Mother's Day came and went, forgotten. Today, I'm thrilled when they call me and remember me. Yet even today, I never forget their birthdays, the days they were born even though I wasn't there.

As a brand-new mother of 18 months, it took some time for me to acclimatize to being a mother of pre-teens, but I was so lucky and blessed that those boys were them. They tested me and taught me love from a different angle. I thank them for that. I couldn't love them more if they were my very own. Their own beautiful children have given me my second most important job in life, next to motherhood: the opportunity to be a grandmother, a nana.

My second marriage gave me our son, Matthew. All my four children are loving and caring individuals, and Matthew is no exception. He is the one who always finds and sends me the most beautiful greeting cards. Thank you, Matthew, for always making the time to remember me. I feel so blessed to be your mother.

There was a time when I wanted another child, but I didn't know if that was going to be possible after my first marriage broke down. Fortunately, I found love again, and we were blessed with Matthew. His name means "gift from God," and to me he was that gift indeed. He is the link that joined us all together, and his two middle names come from the two loves in my life, my dad and his dad. When I say, "I love you more, Matthew" I hope he will always know I love him more than my life itself. I would never hesitate to go into a burning building for him. He has always made my heart smile and swell with pride. Matthew's life made my life truly complete.

I felt we always tried our best to teach all of our children about ambition, kindness, love, compassion and honesty. The oldest and youngest of our four children are, yes, you guessed it, **13** years apart. And now I have grandchildren who truly illuminate my life. Their love is the reward in my life. I couldn't love them more, and I can't wait for more! I think of this Scripture verse when I think of this part of my life: "And now these three remain:

Faith, hope and love. But the greatest of these is love." (1 Corinthians **13:13**)

Chapter 8
The Breast Cancer Journey—
The Visions Return

*In reply Jesus declared, "I tell you the truth,
no one can see the kingdom of God unless he is
born again."*

— John 3:3

*The most beautiful people we have known are
those who have known defeat, known suffering,
known struggle, known loss, and have found their
way out of the depths. These persons have an
appreciation, a sensitivity, and an understanding
of life that fills them with compassion, gentleness,
and a deep loving concern. Beautiful people do
not just happen.*

— Roy and Jane Nichols

Before you hear them, you can never imagine how devastating the words "you have cancer" can be. Cancer, after all, happens to other people. I will always remember that day when the phone rang and I walked across the room to pick up the receiver. I was expecting the doctor's voice but not the words he spoke. Fear made me inconsolable. I was staring death in the face. My world had just turned upside-down. My journey had begun.

Hundreds of emotions run through you when you hear these words, and the biggest one is disbelief. I had read once that everyone has "a day of disaster," and I realized this day was mine. How ironic, I thought: Friday, November **13**, 2009.

You never forget the day your world crumbles apart, but for me, it was also the start of my signs from God. He had resumed His mission with me after **23** years. I didn't quite know that then, but now I feel it was a mission I could no longer ignore, and I know that it is my time to share my story and not keep it to myself. My physical illnesses, disabilities and limitations don't define who I am. My faith and the Divine strength have defined and anchored me through all the setbacks in my life. They haven't stopped me from embarking on a great adventure. Let me explain.

In less than 24 business hours after hearing those words, I was face-to-face with my oncologist. After hearing all the medical jargon, I was booked for surgery **13** days later, which fell on my 51st birthday. My medical team mused that they perhaps could have chosen a different surgery date, but my faith was already starting to boil, and I figured that if they were going to give me a whole new lease on life, it might as well be on my birthday! On that day, I would be born again.

I started praying outside the operating room moments before I was anesthetized. I remembered the poem "Footprints" by Margaret Fishback Powers. It is not a biblical verse, but it was a verse I loved. It was then I asked Jesus to pick me up and carry me. It was then my first vision came back with life-transforming power.

It wasn't what I saw on the ultrasound and mammogram machine that mattered. What mattered was what God said about it and what I believed in my heart God was telling me to do. What you see, feel or hear isn't the final word. You can't be moved by your physical senses or the circumstances around you. You must, of course, listen to your doctors, because God uses them in mighty ways, but when your faith is tested to strengthen it, you must do what you believe in your heart God is telling you to do.

God has a plan, and His plan is our plan. Each day we're given a beautiful gift from Him. While we will pray each day for a miracle, we must live each day as if it is a miracle. And it is.

"Lord," I prayed, "as believers, we trust you completely and pray for your Will to be done. Not ours. We pray for complete and total healing so we can grow old and retire together, travel, and hold hands as we watch our children's lives unfold and grow in front of us, under the setting sun."

Three weeks later, again, we met with the oncologist. It was a difficult meeting; I was beginning to feel vulnerable. It was a feeling I was unfamiliar with. As my doctor delivered the results, I remember feeling totally out of control over the chain of events. He had taken the tumour and two lymphatic nodes, and the pathology report confirmed they had found cancer in the tumour and the one sentinel node.

We now had another choice to make. The doctor suggested further surgery as the best option, to see how much further the cancer had progressed. I was still in the eye of the hurricane. How could this be happening when I never felt anything different? I decided to undergo another surgery, but this time, he would be taking more lymphatic nodes, tissue the size of two golf balls. Although I remained focused on God, this news was horrifying. I collapsed in the room.

I waited for five more weeks, and it was then that I had my second vision. My first vision had been so long ago. I remembered it as different from a dream. It was not muddled, and its meaning was perfectly clear. This vision was different. Instead of watching myself, I was living the message. This vision gave me the inner strength I needed to push forward and fight.

In my vision, I was sitting on what appeared to be a lawn chair on a wooden deck. This deck had no railing, and no other person or being was present. I was all alone, facing backwards. Beyond the deck was a pool of water much like a child's wading pool, which I did not see at the time. All of a sudden, I could feel an enormous force pulling me back into the pool of water. It was like an enormous wind, with a powerful force that was moving me to a place; I was never touched by human hands. I found myself in this pool with about two feet of water above my face.

I felt no panic as you might expect. Rather, there was a feeling of contentment and an all-embracing peace as I stayed there, not fighting to rescue myself. It was like I was calmly floating, but at the same time I was totally immersed in the water. I was not gasping for air or struggling like one would expect from drowning. It was calm, peaceful and serene. It had been 23 years but I never could forget that same ultimate angelic feeling of peace! We really must create a new word for this depth and magnitude of peace because there isn't a word in our current vocabulary which accurately describes it. I remember thinking, "I can give up,"—or rather, give in. Then it occurred to me: Jesus knows us all to the very depths of our souls: all our worries and dreams, all hopes and fears, all goodness and all our weaknesses. He can see our faults and our sins; He wants nothing more than for us to heal our hearts and cleanse our souls so we can love Him as immeasurably as he loves us. It could all end here, with Him, where I felt incredibly safe.

Then, without any warning, as fast as I fell back, I felt that same tremendous force pulling me out—like someone had grabbed hold of my shirt in the front and was yanking me out against my will. I could see no one. I thought to myself, "He obviously is not going to let me give up and make it easy for me!"

As my face left the water, I felt like a bottle being pulled from a sink full of water. You know the sound it makes when the air breaks the suction and it makes that bubble-bursting sound?

My eyes flew wide open, and I was awake. I wasn't gasping like one would expect. I just whispered into the darkness to myself, "I just chose life!" I knew the message immediately. I didn't have to think about the vision for even a second to know what this vision meant. God was telling me I could not give up. He wasn't going to let me. It was not my time. I needed to fight.

I shared this vision with my priest in a private conversation during a visit to receive the sacrament of the Anointing of the Sick. He commented on the common relationship between water and baptism. Water is symbolic of the Holy Spirit when He is manifesting within the life of a believer; Christ compared the infilling of the Spirit to someone with living water flowing from their innermost being (John 7:38). Baptism is just a ceremonial way of washing away "the dirt" (sin) we have accrued on our Earthly journeys. The *Catechism of the Catholic Church* speaks of this when it says, "Baptism gives a share in the common priesthood of all believers" (1268). This is how we can recover our original Heavenly character.

The vision also reminded me of the Scripture from Deuteronomy when Moses tells the people what they must do in order to enter into the Promised Land—obey the commandments of the Lord, love Him, and walk in His ways: "Today, I have given you the choice between life and death, between blessings and curses. I call on Heaven and Earth to witness the choice you make. Oh, that you would choose life, that you and your descendants, might live!"

A week before my second surgery, I approached the pre-op department at the hospital and took a number; all patients are required to take one so everyone is taken in sequence. My eyes widened as I looked at the ticket. I couldn't keep my comments to myself and told the nurse, "This number should never be in the pack." Of course, it was number **13** again.

Up to that point, I was still interpreting its meaning to be bad luck. Little did I know then it meant something entirely different. How ignorant we are sometimes; humans easily believe superstitions instead of trusting God's forever promise and His vow to never leave us.

We kept the lights and decorations that Christmas to the bare minimum. I was doing everything I could to appear in the festive spirit for my family throughout the holidays. As the last car left the driveway, the Christmas tree came down and all the decorations were returned to the boxes under the stairway.

I could only deal with one main event at a time. I also learned to live in the present moment and inhabit one square of the calendar at a time. I was looking forward to the New Year, but my second surgery was going to take place on December 30, 2009, and all I could think about was having another unpleasant surgery.

The second surgery was actually worse than the first, and it took weeks to be rid of its painful reminder and resume my normal life. It was a treat not having to wear blouses that had buttons down the front because of a drain, and it was nice to be able to shower again on my own. Problem was, three weeks later, we had to meet with the oncologist once again for the next round of results. Thank goodness for my faith.

As the oncologist entered the room, he wasted no time delivering his report. He said they had removed 17 more lymphatic nodes from my left underarm, and this time they were all clear! He also said they took more tissue from around the original tumour site, and again, it was all clear. The second surgery revealed no further cancer. "Thanks be to God," I whispered. As the news was still sinking in, I noted that this meant that on my birthday, which had been 13 days after I was told about my cancer, all my cancer had been removed. The number 13 all of a sudden started to sound less threatening to me. How great it was to be given a new lease on life on my birthday.

Just as I started to enjoy this last news, I was hit with another thunderbolt. Two new specialists entered the room, and they started to review their recommendations for preventative chemotherapy and radiation cancer treatment. It was another thing to get my head around. I was going to be taken down to my knees. I was about to lose every hair on my entire body while being injected with the most powerful drugs known to mankind. Every fibre of my body was about to be challenged. Cancer was the villain, and death was possible, so I had no choice but to go through it for however long it took; hopefully, I'd survive and win.

On February 5, 2010, I stepped into the boxing ring for the first time for 6 rounds over 18 weeks. I'll never forget that day; I couldn't stop shaking. Fear is one of the toughest emotions to break free from.

Normally, you are allowed one person to accompany you in the chemotherapy room, but this day my husband was on one side of me, and my counselor was on the other. They were both there for two rounds, three weeks apart.

On that first day, I saw a young man, barely 18 years of age, starting his treatments for the first time. Only he was throwing up. My heart bled for him as tears rolled down my face. "There is always someone in this world going through something worse," I thought. This also could have been one of my children instead of me!

All of a sudden, my strength started to kick in, but don't let anyone ever tell you it is easy. It isn't, but it's a lot easier with Christ by your side. I kept thinking about the vision in the pool of water. It kept me focused and reminded me of God's plan for me.

By now, my teeth were even starting to break, a reminder of the wear and tear that cancer was taking on my body. I started to grit my teeth so much at night with the stress. My dentist eventually made me a bite guard to save my teeth from further destruction.

My chemotherapy treatment was described as Third Generation. In simple terms, this means I was in line for the third type of cocktail known to beat this beast. It consisted of three types of drugs for the first three rounds and three different types of drugs for the last three rounds. The most difficult part of each of the six chemotherapy sessions was the administration of the needles, because the first strike doesn't always turn out to be a home run. It took many times and many tries before the implantation of the IV hit a good vein.

With each try, the frustration and seriousness of my decisions became more and more clear. Chemotherapy has rules, just like baseball. One rule was that if one nurse struck out twice, another nurse came to bat. During one round, it took more than three strikes. It took a full four turns at bat. The only thing that made me smile that day was another brave man who was "on my same team." He was sitting across from me, smiling back and nodding, telling me he understood and shared my pain. You really never know how strong you are until forcing yourself to be strong is the only choice you have.

As I continued to tremble, they injected a red solution into my bloodstream. It was called Epirubicin (e-pee-ROO-bi-sin). This was the drug I feared the most. It was the drug that all cancer patients feared—the blood red cocktail that took away your dignity, made you lose your hair and announced to the outside world, "I have cancer."

A faith filled cancer survivor gave me some very valuable advice on how to confront my fears about chemotherapy. They said, "As the hospital is administering this drug into your veins, you may want to think of it as Christ's blood and let yourself accept and get through it with His help. Truthfully, for me, this was the best and only calming advice I was given. It was then I really felt His presence. The Lord instantly blessed me with an awesome peace. Knowing I was in good hands, whether I lived or died, kept me from plunging into depression and kept me strong.

God was working His miracle through the doctors. With each round, I reminded myself it was like my trip to the desert. I would picture a desert, even though a desert can be a scary place. We don't like a place to be desolate and dry, hot, and lacking the bare essentials of life, like water and food. We like our surroundings to be flowers, pillows, rainbows and comfort.

But sometimes life is like the desert. We all have desert experiences at some time in our lives. Surprisingly, during those times in our desert, we experience the greatest growth in our spiritual lives. These are the times we are tested, and we can grow in grace and love and come out on the other side as better people and better Christians.

In parallel, in the Bible, after being baptized, Jesus fasted for 40 days and nights in the Judaean Desert. During this time, Satan appeared to Jesus and tried to tempt him.

With Jesus having refused each temptation, the devil then departed, and Jesus returned to Galilee.

I focused on the saying "If God brings you to it, He'll bring you through it." Around this time, I tried my hand at oil painting, and I painted a picture that placed myself in the centre of my journey. It showed me going through all the seasons, with Christ's light as my focus. It reminded me of what cancer cannot do. It cannot cripple love, shatter hope, corrode faith, destroy peace, kill friendship, suppress memories, silence courage, invade the soul, steal eternal life or conquer the Spirit.

Instead of interpreting the big *C* as *cancer,* I chose to take its definition to an even a higher level and think of the big *C* as *Christ.* The scars now forever imprinted on my body, I felt God say, were the marks of my suffering and a remembrance of how He had healed and restored me. Scars tell stories. Scars mean strength and survival. Scars mean you showed up for the fight instead of running from it. It means the hurt is over and the wound is closed. It means you conquered the pain, learned the lesson, grew stronger and moved forward. Hopefully the scars and the fear won't hold you hostage. And we've all got them, inside and out. We are all bravely fighting our own battle, defending our own front line, struggling in our own way.

Rumi, a **13**th century Persian poet, one of the world's brightest creative talents, on par with Beethoven, Shakespeare and Mozart, once said, "The wound is the place where the Light enters you." After all, Jesus suffered and was brutally beaten. And He still carries the scars from His crucifixion on His side, His hands and His feet as a mark of love for us.

I met some wonderful friends while in a counseling group at the hospital's Cancer Clinic. One elderly woman, named Pat, stood out from the rest, and we later continued our friendship. She was a dear and sweet person, and she often reminded me of the first day we met and how my presence made her feel when I stepped into the room. She always called me Katie, and, of all things, she referred to me as "an angel." She said it was hard to put into words, but she felt a warm glow every time she looked at me. She said I shone and she was always drawn to me. "It was a feeling," she said, that "radiated from" me, drawing her immediately close to me. My sensitivity, my smile and my words comforted her; she never felt that from anyone else in the room, even the facilitator. She said she could tell that I had an enormous heart, with a lot of love to go around, and I seemed to be extra aware of other people's feelings. She said the level of empathy I possessed was special, and it was appreciated by others around me.

A couple of years later, when I visited her in a nursing home, she cried as she told me of her husband's passing. I told her my stories and reminded her to have faith in our Lord Jesus Christ. When I think of it now, I really never asked her about her religion or if she believed, but to me, it didn't matter, because her openness made me feel she was one of God's chosen people.

I told her that her husband, Bob, would be waiting for her, like Frank was waiting for my mother-in-law when it was time. Only Jesus knows when that time will be, so she needed to fulfill her purpose in life. I told her that lots of people loved and needed her at that moment, so that must have been why she was still with us. The next visit, I popped in to see her with my husband, John. I brought with me a box of homemade Valentine cookies. I was happy she was finally able to meet John, to whom she had spoken on the telephone briefly many times.

One day, I gave her a small crucifix after John and I had returned from our trip to Jerusalem. I told her that I had prayed for her in some special places, and she cried, telling me she was so moved I had remembered her so far away.

I smiled, watching her hands clutch the small crucifix as I left that day. I told her that I believed God needed me to do His work, to reassure people like her. If only it were that easy to place Jesus in people's hands!

On a recent visit to see Pat she astonished me by taking it up one more notch. In the middle of our delightful conversation, she looked in my eyes and asked me, "Have you been chosen?" Never had I ever before been left so totally speechless.

During my recovery, John and I continued, each night, to read the Bible he had bought for me for Christmas. It was the New International Version, and all of Jesus's words were written in red print. John would read it to me, and we would share this special time together, reflecting on God's word. This brought a sense of tranquility into our world, one that for so long seemed turned upside-down.

Getting to *know* Jesus became something different from knowing *about* Jesus—not just facts and figures but what He had done for *me*. We not only read and became familiar with Scripture; we also developed a deep, personal, committed relationship with Him that reminded me that He was accompanying me through this journey. I didn't feel alone.

During the course of 18 weeks, life showed no kindness. Each week brought on all the symptoms the doctors had warned me about. I had read all the brochures outlining all the possible side effects that could happen; many of them fell true. Nurses came to the house within 12 hours of each chemotherapy treatment to inject me with fever-reducing drugs. I lay in bed, sick from the drugs that were supposed to prevent me from being sick. Nail roots died, and hair fell out.

During one round, I fell in the parking lot going into the treatment centre, and that presented a whole new array of X-rays and complications. I spent three hours in emergency having X-rays done before they could even move me back to the Cancer Treatment Centre to continue that day's treatments. I broke my glasses, and as I started the last three rounds of treatment, I had to wrap my hands and feet with ice packs. The ice was to prevent the nail roots from dying, which happened anyway. On that day, it was hard to tell which ice packs were from the fall and which were for the treatment! The journey continued, but I knew God never sends anyone into a situation alone. I was confident He was standing beside me every step of the way.

I neared completion of the chemotherapy and was beginning to start to prepare myself for the next five weeks of daily radiation. It was then I encountered my next vision, only this vision came from a very dark place.

After reading my Bible and settling into sleep for the evening, I closed my eyes. As the dark side absorbed my soul, I felt an enormous and furious push-and-pull struggle from within. I could not open my eyes. The closest description in my mind that matched the sounds was like that of a vicious tiger or an angry, ferocious, fiery dragon. I could hear gnarling and intense, outraged behaviour far beyond anything I'd seen from the most dangerous and upset animal.

I couldn't see what I perceived as animals, but I could hear and feel the blood-curdling gnashing of teeth and the intolerable animosity they had toward each other. The noise was terrifying. Somehow, I knew their violent battle was a matter of life and death, and I knew they weren't going to stop until one succeeded in overtaking the other. Although I could not see them, I knew I was close to them; I could feel the intense heat of their breath without feeling burned.

It was like being blindfolded and locked in a dark room with ferocious, life-threatening, evil creatures or beasts that you could only imagine were dinosaur- or dragon-sized;

they were violent and angry, and they were so close, it would make the hairs on the back of your neck stand up. I felt both heat and chill at the same time.

During this moment of truth, I could hear and feel them but not see them. At the same time, I felt a presence that was both encouraging and calming. Up until this point, I couldn't even pry my eyes open, even if I'd wanted to. A force was keeping the real vision from me.

The heat of the fire and the intensity around me was much too great for my mind to absorb. When I was finally able to open my eyes, I clearly knew the message.

God had pulled the cancer from me! He had fought Satan to keep me in this world. I lay there, numb, for what seemed an eternity. I was frozen, motionless, terrified to move even a muscle; I lay there, straining, peering into the darkness, hoping to catch a glimpse of what may have still been lurking.

Deep down, I was really afraid. At the same time, I really wanted to see—perhaps it was just human curiosity. But I likely wasn't meant to see them, as they now were gone, and my world was transformed into a place of incredible stillness. I didn't feel the indescribable peace this time. I only felt an incredible stillness.

It wasn't until I returned to Mass, two days later, that I was able to put some perspective on what had transpired in that darkness. As I was listening to our priest's homily, I heard him reiterate how time and time again, Jesus healed the sick. He described the act as removing the "demons."

Those words pierced me like a sword. Yes, the presence of that tiger or dragon or whatever it was I sensed had been inches from me in the room that night. It had the characteristics of fierce demons putting up an epic struggle. A presence made itself known to me and "saved me from the demons." I could feel three of us present.

Demons are fallen angels, angels who rebelled against God. Demons are evil, deceptive and destructive. Demons masquerade as "angels of light" and as "servants of righteousness" (2 Corinthians 11:14–15).

I should have known: When we invite and rely on the strength of Jesus, victory is assured against Satan in every spiritual battle.

If you remember our Gospel reading from Matthew 17, when Jesus discovered His disciples could not drive out a demon from a man's son, Jesus took care of it Himself. When the disciples asked Him why they couldn't do it, Jesus replied, "Because of your little faith. Amen, I say to you, if you have faith the size of a mustard seed, you will say to this mountain, 'Move from here to there,' and it will move."

For faith is very powerful. Mountains can be many things in our lives that make us doubt, and we find it so hard to move out of the way. Jealousy, lust, greed, anger, addiction—pick one weighing on you—but don't let the size of the mountain discourage you. To be human is to at times doubt even the most basic elements of our faith. In fact, doubt can be an instrument for the building of faith. Persist in prayer to obtain the depth of faith that is necessary. I've personally seen it defeat demons!

This vision provided me with three lessons.

First, the message reassured me that God is never far from any one of us. It is sometimes very hard for us to remember God is always near. During those times, when we drift away from God, He remains near us. It could be that our backs are turned, or maybe we're not looking for Him at all. And when we are seeking Him and can't seem to find Him, it is our lack of vision. So often we cannot see through our own anguish, suffering or hurt. We can be blinded by our pain, but you will find Him if you really open your heart. Jesus, in fact, told His disciples to remember the bigger picture when He told them that they would be put to death, but not a hair on their heads would be destroyed. Jesus understood that on this Earth, our bodies are temporary, and perseverance on this planet will secure our lives for eternity.

Second, the vision provided me with the hope that God fulfills His promises to us. And third, it provided me with the reassurance we are left on this Earth until we have fulfilled our purpose and we have learned all we need to learn here. Perhaps that's the time we earn our wings and become angels.

I don't believe God creates cancer or other illness. I believe they come from our environment and the results of our broken world. I do believe in healing, in a purpose for our lives, and that there is "a time to die and return, as we are not supposed to change God's holy ordinance."

Fortunately for me, the doctors tell me my surgery and treatments were successful. Apart from their residual effects, I still suffer chest spasms, collapsed veins, anxiety and lymphedema. DNA testing recommended a cancer drug to continue for a total of 10 years, but in the big picture, I thank God every day for the blessing of being cancer-free. I'll never forget or be able to thank the countless number of people who sent me cards, letters, flowers or memento's, made a telephone call, drove me or accompanied me somewhere, or visited and supported me in some way during my journey including the nurses and doctors. Your love and caring support was a sure sign of hope in humanity and every act of kindness was deeply appreciated from each and every one of you. I will never forget that time in my life. The day I left work the calendar on my cubicle wall displayed 2009. The day I returned I replaced it with a calendar for 2011. Although it is often called "a journey" I remember feeling like I lost a whole year somewhere. Looking back, I actually found myself in that year and the light that was shed only left me self-assured.

I know there are sceptical people, including my own brother, who often like to challenge me with those difficult questions like "Okay, where do you think Heaven is?" By trying to make an absolute statement on where the spiritual world could be, we are setting limits on a subject no one really knows for sure.

One of the best New Age answers I have heard to "Where is Heaven?" is "Where is the Internet?" Although we cannot give the Internet a geographical location, we know it exists. Why can't this also be true for Heaven?

I do find it fascinating to hear how many people report visions and near-death experiences that are similar when describing the "Other Side." Eben Alexander, MD, a neurosurgeon who wrote *Proof of Heaven,* would be the first to argue that the afterlife is not a fantasy produced by the brain under extreme stress; he had his own NDE and medical-miracle recovery. Raymond A. Moody, Jr., MD, PhD, author of *Life after Life* says, "Dr. Eben Alexander's near-death experience is the most astounding I have heard in more than four decades of studying this phenomenon." In Moody's words, Eben "is living proof of an afterlife."

In Luke 20, Jesus explains what Heaven would be like after the resurrection. He says, "They neither marry nor are given in marriage. They can no longer die, for they are like angels."

According to Jesus, we won't have any need to marry or engage in other relationships like we do now, because we will be able to love everyone perfectly. And because Heaven is Love, unconditional love binds us to those we have shared unconditional love with, and we also benefit from true love, which knows no boundaries.

Dr. James Merritt sums it up when he says: "The Greatest Man in history is Jesus. He had no servants, yet they called

Him Master. He had no degree, yet they called Him Teacher. He had no medicines, yet they called Him Healer. He had no army, yet kings feared Him. He won no military battles, yet He conquered the world. He committed no crime, yet they crucified Him. He was buried in a tomb, yet He lives today."

I've especially always liked what Matthew Kelly says: "Who did Jesus claim to be? He claimed to be the Son of God. If he isn't the Son of God, he's not a great prophet, he's not a great teacher, he is the biggest liar in the history of the world." Satan, on the other hand, cannot be trusted and has proven to be the author of all lies and the keeper of eternal darkness.

The cancer radiation treatment did make me feel like I was in that eternal darkness. Every day for five weeks, I drove to the hospital to lie on the table, allowing rays to sear and burn my body. The small dots they tattooed on my chest kept the rays aligned with each treatment. It is hard to know the best possible way to physically overcome this disease, but you have to make what you think are the best possible decisions at the time. With those decisions, I trusted in God.

Chapter 9
The Accident

Pain makes you think. Thinking makes you wise.
Wisdom makes you free.

—Unknown

Do not forget to entertain strangers for by so
doing, some people have entertained angels
without knowing it.

—Hebrews 13:2

When you think you have gone through everything you possibly can, life can always throw another hardball in your direction. At these times, we are tempted to question God and lose faith. But these are the times you should never lose faith; you should gain more. It's always easier to give up than to keep fighting. I am no exception to this rule. I've felt like giving up plenty of times, but faith has taught me that even though a rising number of people are eschewing faith and religion, there is always another side.

It was a stormy night, and the winds were blowing at a great speed. The sky was dark, and although the rains hadn't started yet, it seemed like a night one should stay home and find a nice, safe, dry, warm place to sit with a good book. (There wasn't even any point looking for a good movie, as the satellite connection was about to go down.)

I was just starting to feel more like myself, with the last of my cancer treatments now behind me, and my hair had finally reached the "acceptable" status. I had come home from the hair salon and had asked my husband to take a photograph of me, as I had been recording each milestone for what seemed like an eternity.

Despite the inclement weather, we decided to go out because a client of my husband's had passed away from breast cancer, and we wanted to pay our respects at the funeral home visitation. Because I had met Carole a couple times at the Cancer Clinic and had admired her courageous battle, I felt an enormous desire to pay her tribute alongside my husband. It was the night of August 24, 2011.

We rushed to the car, being buffeted by gales, and drove along, watching dark clouds billow in the sky. It was a strange and terrifying night. I suppose the summer heat drove these clouds into confusion, and I could feel the sky erupting in anger. To me, it reminded me of my own epic struggle. I remember silently asking God to take the burden of anger and sadness away and to replace it and fill my heart with Christ's peace and understanding.

My husband tried to brighten up the mood that evening on our way back home. He asked me if ice cream was in order, so we stopped at an ice cream parlour only blocks away from the sad place we had just left. As I sat in the car, he came back out and shielded himself from the high winds as he balanced two treats. We sat there for a moment, indulging and remembered Carole. We commented on how lucky we were as we counted our blessings. As John started the car, I fed my ice cream cone through the seatbelt, locking the buckle with my free left hand. It was time to venture home before the downpour let loose.

As we headed towards the exit, I could see a car way up on the hill. I also noticed the black threatening clouds forming above us. As we pulled out of the driveway, all I could hear was a loud explosion. It sounded like a bomb had just gone off, and my mind hadn't yet caught up with reality. In what seemed like slow motion, I could see the metal door frame twisting and turning as the metal screamed and screeched into a new dimension. It gave brand-new meaning to the word *transformers*.

My head was thrown to the right as window glass came back into my mouth. The glove compartment became unlatched and smacked my knees, and the passenger door took on the shape of the other car's front bumper. It missed my legs by a fraction of a centimetre. The ice cream cones disappeared in an instant. (We found them the next day, smeared onto the back window and on one of the backseat armrests.)

Our car made a 90-degree turn as the impact drove the car around in the opposite direction before it came to a screeching halt. All I could do was quiver; the pain I already felt in my head was more than I could stand. I looked over at John and kept saying, "I'm just not supposed to be here."

He asked me if I was okay, and then he said, "No, you are wrong. It's the opposite. You *are* supposed to be here."

A man stuck his head in the window and said, "Are you okay? Hang on, I've just called an ambulance." As I was begging for ice for my head, I could hear the rescue sirens coming in our direction; it seemed like hours before the emergency vehicles arrived.

The driver who had hit us was now quite a distance way. Although his air bag had inflated, he suffered no injuries. He told my husband he hadn't seen us at the time of the accident because he'd been busy watching the dark clouds forming behind him in his rear view mirror. He'd been going too fast to stop.

Moments later, a fireman was in the backseat, asking me questions and trying to keep me conscious while the other firemen used the Jaws of Life to remove the passenger door.

Every day, I thank God for sending His guardian angels to nudge me to place my seatbelt back on only seconds before the impact. If it weren't for that seatbelt, I would have been thrown through the windshield and undoubtedly killed in that crash. I had just escaped the next bullet fired after fighting cancer.

The next day when I shared the story on the phone with my father, I heard him say, "I'm glad you didn't call me last night. I'm glad you waited to call me today once you were home and could tell me you were okay." I don't think he could have handled losing a child that day—especially at his age of 82 years.

The next picture I placed in the milestone photograph book didn't show me with a new hairstyle; it showed me with a right black eye. What it didn't show was the inside of my head, which was rocked by a major trauma (a concussion) and whiplash—two conditions that set my healing back an entire year.

Cars can be written off, but people can't. But guess what! I wasn't in that funeral home, and I was still alive! Thanks be to God, yet again. Life is all how you look at it. I could be feeling sorry for myself or question God, but I choose to count it as yet another blessing. I truly believe if we never suffer pain or grief in this world, we would never understand the true meaning of happiness or appreciate why we are here. There are blessings hidden in every struggle you face, but you must be willing to open your heart and mind to see them. Grief itself never ends, but it changes with time. It's a passage, not a place to stay. Grief is not a sign of weakness or a lack of faith, but I'd like to think of it as "a blessing" or "a lesson." Grief is truly the price of love.

Now, this is where it gets better, my friend. Buckle your seatbelt!

It was three days after this accident, on August 27, 2011. Upon retiring for the night, I picked up my grandmother's photograph, which was sitting on my night table beside my bed.

In a conversation with my mother earlier that day, she asked me if any of my teeth had been smashed in the accident. Fortunately, they were not. She then continued to comment on her mother's teeth, saying how I must take after her mother, who had beautiful teeth. I was used to this kind of conversation in our home about my teeth because it was common knowledge I had nice teeth; I had made it 50 years without a cavity, and this always seemed to arouse discussion.

When I set the photograph down on the night table, I turned off the lamp that was also sitting there. As I turned into bed, all of a sudden I could still see a light over my head, but it was slightly back from my view so that I could see only a glow. I leaned back, and I could feel the glow follow me in the direction I was leaning. I then leaned forward, and again it followed. (The rebel in me made the thought of trying to trick these things, seem normal.)

John was lying beside me with his eyes closed. "There is a light over my head," I told him.

"It must be your halo," he said, half-kidding. At the precise moment he spoke, he opened his eyes and looked over at me. The glow disappeared. I truly think I was the only one who was meant to see it. You might suggest this was the result of my head trauma, but I remain unconvinced. I saw the light; it was there.

For the next several nights, I tried to re-enact the experience by performing the same repetitive actions after

I turned in for the night, but I could not see the same special light. Have you ever had an incident where there wasn't any explanation that made sense? This was one of those most powerful and confirming incidents I'd ever witnessed. In my mind, only a spiritual explanation describes it like a hand fitting a glove.

It made me wonder if I had a guardian angel over my head. What if my grandmother Rose was my guardian angel, as my mother and I had talked about her only moments before? "Makes sense," I thought, because she was the person in my life who'd had the most angelic qualities and she always told me how much she loved the Lord. Did that circular aura of light have anything to do with her, or was I visited by Divine intervention? Whatever it was, I believe I was still meant to be here to tell you about it.

I believe there are angels all around us, nudging us forward and backward and even sideways. These angels may or may not have wings, but they appear in our lives as messengers, and they come forth in forms we can and will accept. I think we may even have "personal angels" to help guide us every day, all day. Angels want us to follow the path that has been laid out for us by our loving God, and this could be the reason for all the so-called "coincidences."

Before I end this chapter, I'd like to tell you about a story I once heard about an angel. The story involved a woman who was a nurse who worked in a hospice centre. She was a cradle Catholic, which means a person who has been raised in the Catholic faith since birth (in contrast to a person who has converted to the faith). She had apparently participated regularly in the faith until she was 16 years old but had never attended church any Sunday after that—or any Christmas, Easter, wedding, funeral or even an occasional Mass. She said the last 22 years, she worked on Sundays, but she had fallen away from the Church for a total of 40 years. That was, until "the angel" . . .

One day, she was visiting a hospice patient under her care who was dying. The person told her they had been visited by an angel. This angel told the dying person they were going to pass at 7:**13**. After hearing the comment, the nurse told a colleague if this turned out to be true, it would be enough to return her back to her religion. She commented that the family seemed curious if 7:**13** meant a.m. or p.m., so for a while it was quite hard on the family as they patiently wondered and watched their loved one in the last days. Then, on July **13**, their loved one passed. It turned out 7:**13** meant July **13**. It wasn't what they'd originally assumed, but it was what the angel had promised. It was on that day the hospice nurse returned to practising her faith on a regular basis once again after 40 years. I truly thank this nurse and this family for this beautiful story. I hope by sharing it in this book, it helps that angel continue to live out the message.

There truly are so many unexplainable stories in this world, and there are so many things we just don't know or have simple answers for. Sometimes, you just don't know what you don't know.

When I first heard of this remarkable, moving story, I was fascinated but not surprised about the story's numbers and sequences. I will talk about this in Chapter **13**.

Chapter 10
The Warning:
Leaving My Life but Not My Heart

*"Then I heard a holy one speaking, and another
holy one said to him, "How long will it take for
the vision to be fulfilled—the vision concerning
the daily sacrifice, the rebellion that causes deso-
lation, and the surrender of the sanctuary and of
the host that will be trampled underfoot?"*

*He said to me, "It will take 2,300 eve-
nings and mornings; then the sanctuary will
be reconsecrated."*

—Daniel 8:13-14

The Prophet Daniel, identified as one of the four main
Prophets from the Hebrew Scriptures, can perhaps
best be described as a "seer", a man of visions. The Book
is filled with the dreams and visions of Daniel concerning
future events. Scholars today still continue to debate what
category this *Book of Daniel* should fall under: prophecy,
wisdom literature, or even apocalyptic literature.

Like Daniel, I've had dreams and visions pass through my mind while lying on my bed and I've written down their substance. They too consisted of great winds, great beasts and the Almighty, the "Alpha" and the "Omega", (the first and last letters of the Greek alphabet, proclaiming Christ as *the beginning and the end.*)

For me, all of my visions have occurred at certain times in my life, but none of them occurred on a monumental date or a repetitive date—except for "the warning," which in hindsight, could be interpreted as the beginning and the end.

On the night of New Year's Eve, December 31, 2011, I awoke and sat bolt upright, trembling. Two of the saddest days of my life had played out in visions before me. I wasn't shown *how* they would happen, but I awoke knowing they were close and they *were* going to happen.

I was told I was going to lose my dearly beloved father and my most faithful and devoted loving friend, who had also remained by my side throughout my cancer journey— my cat, Nike. How could I go on without one or the other?

I thought it must be because Dad had recently taken care of Nike for us, when we went off to Italy for three weeks, only four months before. Maybe they both were playing on my mind, and I thought of them spending time together. Regardless, I was so shaken and, although some dreams never connect or make any kind of sense, this one felt real.

The next morning, Nike approached me on the bed for her early morning pat and I thought, "Oh, thank God! It was only a dream. Today, they are both still with me. But why, on the first day of a brand-new year, did I see an event so clearly?"

Did this dream represent a way to cope with that fear and the reality of time coming to pass? Was it setting the stage for this brand new year?

From many conversations I've had with God, I knew God never gives us more than we can handle. I also knew He understood the kind of love I had for my father. After all, I reminded myself, Jesus loved His Father like I do, and He knew and understood this deep love.

I thought many times, "Does this mean this year is about to drastically change, and God is helping to prepare me?"

I already knew God could use dreams to speak to us. He did it in the Bible, and He is still doing this every day. When a believer experiences a spiritual dream in which the meaning is veiled, the dream can be understood by using the Scriptures to interpret the symbolism. This time I knew its meaning, and this time it wasn't complicated. He was preparing my heart to understand there is a time for everything, and this time, He was preparing me to accept His Will.

Dad always checked the local newspaper, seven days a week, for his own obituary. I never could really understand why people do that, but since he told me this, I've heard several elderly people I know do the same. Perhaps it is their way of accepting that one day all things in this lifetime must come to an end.

One day, he saw his name, but it was another person with the identical name from another family. A few days passed after this incident, and Dad told me he had seen someone he knew in the grocery store. "Gee, I read you had died," said the man. "Good to see it wasn't you."

Sometime later, when Dad made an appointment at a doctor's office, he also found out his doctor had removed his file from their records! What's that saying . . . "Be careful what you wish for"? I know for a fact Dad wasn't wishing—it was quite the opposite—but he was amazed at how many years he was given compared to most others.

The day Dad's obituary did appear in the local newspaper, it was monumental for my 85-year-old mother.

She described the scene to me. The obituary was really supposed to have been listed in the local paper two days before, on Saturday, but for some reason the newspaper didn't put it in on time. When it missed the Saturday paper, she had called, and they had agreed to post it in two editions following Saturday.

As Mom opened the paper, sitting with her cup of tea, her eyes focused on the Obituary section. She had the light above the table where she was sitting turned on. As soon as her eyes fixated on Dad's name, the light went out, and the power to the microwave clock went off for about four seconds.

Mom said her heart was in her mouth, and she looked up and immediately said, "Is that you, Bob? Are you here?" She could still hear the low hum of the refrigerator, and every other light source remained on in the apartment. She said she had to reset the clock on the microwave later, as it totally went blank. She said, "Honest to God as my witness, you would have never believed it."

Later that week, she also told me, a gold mantle clock, which was sitting on a small portable fireplace close to Dad's chair, had also stopped, and she was frustrated that she could not get it working. That same gold mantle clock has never restarted again.

The day after Dad's funeral, my mother said she had fallen asleep in her chair, and she awoke feeling disoriented. As she opened her eyes, for a split second, she saw my dad across the room sitting in "his chair." It was like a quick flash. Even my mother believes his spirit is around us.

I read, years ago, this happens when spirits are present—that clocks stop. I also heard we are given a choice at the time of our death to return on Earth to comfort loved ones, for a short time, by remaining to help their spirits heal. I'm not talking about evil or wicked spirits but angelic spirits.

Eight weeks after my father's death, on June 8, 2013, my mother reported yet another strange event. She was doing some laundry. When she walked into the bedroom to put away some clothes, she noticed my father's clock on his night table had stopped. She looked over at her night table, and the clock that was sitting there was still going. She thought, "How can this be? These clocks are both on the same electrical line." She walked out of the bedroom and down the hallway, back to the kitchen, and sure enough, the clock on the microwave was out again. No other clocks in the apartment had stopped.

Three days later, on June 11, she noticed the kitchen clock had stopped and another mantle clock had also started to act up. It was the mantle clock Dad had taken to get serviced only a year or so before his death. It had been working totally fine up until the day Dad passed, April 18, 2013. Since then, it has started to chime one less chime on each hour. If it was four o'clock, it would only chime three times. How strange.

Twice now, his clock on his night table and the micro-wave clock stopped in sync again. I asked Mom if all the clocks did this when Dad was there, and she stared at me and said, "Never."

She said, "You know, in my grief, I've been saying, 'Why did you leave me?' And when things haven't gone right, I've called out to your Dad and asked him to 'help me.' I wonder if he is still here."

After my first vision and the research I did **23** years ago, something tells me Dad's spirit remained, lingering, and his spirit was making all time in that apartment stand still during the first year of his absence.

Since reading Raymond Moody's book, I found recent research by Dr. Peter Fenwick that included analysis of more than 300 examples of healthy people who had wit-nessed near-death experiences. It found that many people associated with a dying person who was emotionally close to them reported occurrences of clocks stopping and electrical devices spontaneously switching themselves on or malfunctioning in some way. (Dr. Peter Fenwick's death bed phenomena) "All the phenomena which occur around the time of death or at the moment of death suggest that consciousness may exist beyond the brain and that communication between two people who are emotionally close but far apart is a possibility," said Fenwick in an interview.

Personally, I believe the soul leaves the body at the moment of death, not that the body's physical death is determined by when the soul departs. This would account for all the near-death experiences that people describe of their souls leaving their bodies before or after being physically pronounced dead. I also believe a soul is returned back to the body by God if the person's purpose in life has yet to be fulfilled. If it is time to return to God, I believe the soul leaves the body, never to return. I've read reported cases saying the soul leaves through the top of the head.

* * *

Port Stanley is a quaint village located on the north shore of Lake Erie at the mouth of Kettle Creek. In the early 1900's, Port Stanley was the main tourist attraction on the lake and was called "The Coney Island of the Great Lakes." The large sandy beach housed a cafeteria, an incline railway to Picnic Hill (which over looked the harbour), a casino, The Stork Club (with a public pool), an outdoor theatre, a Ferris wheel and a rollercoaster. Mackies (a well-known eatery famous for its orangeade and fries) has been on the beach since 1911. Today, it offers a rich history, superb dining, comfortable accommodations, a lift bridge across Kettle Creek, a marina and fish market, restaurants, boutiques, the Port Stanley Festival Theatre, and the Port Stanley Rail Terminal which still operates a tourist train between Sparta and Port Stanley. John and I took our son, Matthew, and his friends there for a birthday party many years ago.

The village was well known in 1926 for a building opened as the L&PS Pavilion, later renamed the Stork Club. This is not to be confused with the famous New York establishment, but it had a **13**,000-square-foot dance floor, the largest dance floor in London or Port Stanley. The club was famous for New Year's Eve celebrations, swing dances and big bands, including Guy Lombardo's; it attracted several famous names to play there.

Both our parents had talked about going there, and what a great place it once was. In 1973, it was closed by health authorities because it could not earn the revenue to keep the building up. H. J. McManus, a London business-man, bought it, and his son, Joe, Jr., led the renovations, reopening it in 1974 with the Harry James Orchestra per-forming before a sellout crowd. The last event was a per-formance by Day Break on New Year's Eve of 1978/1979. A fire in a dumpster 12 days later damaged the building too heavily to save it. I never had the pleasure of experiencing this venue first-hand in its day and only heard countless recollected stories.

Port Stanley was a settlement originally named Kettle Creek. It was founded in 1812 by Lieutenant-Colonel John Bostwick. Around 1824, it was renamed Port Stanley after Edward Smith-Stanley, 14th Earl of Derby, who had visited nearby Port Talbot. Lord Stanley later became the Prime Minister of the United Kingdom. He was the father of Frederick Stanley, 16th Earl of Derby, Governor General of Canada, but he was likely better known as an ice hockey enthusiast and donor of the Stanley Cup in 1893.

This was a place where my dad spent time as a child, as he did later in life. I have a photograph of him there as a baby, with his brother and sister. He told me that as a small child, he fell down the hill and split his head open there.

In the last few years, John and I would ask Mom and Dad if they would like to accompany us for a drive and for a famous waffle cone at Broderick's Ice Cream Parlour, located now on the main street. Dad always loved ice cream and would rarely turn down an opportunity to have some.

We would begin our short stroll as we all indulged in our favourite flavours. The smell of the homemade waffle cone was so pleasant to the senses. We would head to a nearby park, where the channel narrowed and where the lift bridge would let the sail boats through.

On a Saturday afternoon, four months after my dad's passing, John and I took a drive to Port Stanley before church service. We found a rock and sat quietly watching the lake. I could feel all the different memories of each of us floating in the breeze. I started to talk about Dad, and as I did, a gaggle of Canadian geese came out of nowhere and started swimming toward us. As I took the last bite of my cone, I walked along and counted them...**13**.

Two hours later, while sitting in Mass, I started to think about the geese, the warning I'd had on New Year's Eve, and the Stork Club village we had visited that afternoon. As Mass was ending the choir started to sing, and tears flowed down my cheeks. It was Dad's favourite hymn, *You Are Mine*. Was all this linked for me to connect the dots? I'd like to believe so because the similarities and the number 13 seems to keep coming my way.

I think life is like that, but the only way you notice is when you allow yourself to slow your world down and stop to connect the dots.

Chapter 11
The Beacon in the Desert—
The Holy Land

*Jesus answered, "I tell you the truth, no one can
enter the kingdom of God unless he is born of
water and the Spirit. Flesh gives birth to flesh, but
the Spirit gives birth to Spirit."*

—John 3:5

There wasn't anything more common than their surname. But the Smiths were anything but ordinary. We have had a genuine friendship and bonded over a long period of time. Our children all grew up together and each visit was rotated, celebrated and made special. It is, indeed, a special and rare friendship.

Even our children often commented on how we all seemed more deeply rooted, rather more like family than friends. Our friendship had that "play together, pray together" kind of relationship. We were a close, caring and loving group of people, and we shared the same core values. Our children and our pets changed, and our families and our homes changed, and with it all, we shared the ups and downs, in laughter and tears, all of our lives. After our children left the nests and moved forward with their own lives, we decided it was time to create some new experiences and memories.

As I sat quietly in the church pews, my concentration on the homily wandered, and I started contemplating our next adventure. We were leaving the next day with the Smith's for a cruise through the Baltic countries. From what I could tell, our priest was talking about a stained glass window somewhere with inordinate significance, but the word **13** was what awakened me and drew my attention suddenly towards him.

Now wide awake, I anxiously waited to hear another clue about what this **13** was hinting towards. "Please forgive me for my wandering thoughts, dear Lord, and reveal to me what my prayers have been asking you," I thought.

It was then I heard his words like a call of awakening: "Twelve disciples and Christ makes **13**." It was in that moment I realized what my faith had been telling me all along, with no trace of doubt or superstition.

The doubt flew out the window as our flight took us once more across the Atlantic Ocean.

Two days later, as I stood in line for boarding at the cruise line's terminal, I was surrounded by thousands of other passengers who all had quite obviously had the same idea as the four of us. We inched our way through the ropes, holding our passports and paperwork, and we approached 24 customer service counters. We finally arrived at the front of the line. The Smiths walked ahead of us and, as they headed towards their registration counter, I heard our counter number being called, and so did Janet Smith. She turned around and glared at me. She'd also heard them call **13**, and I could read her lips as she mouthed the words, "I don't believe it!" Again, I was right where I was supposed to be, I thought.

The rest of the trip seemed to progress pretty much to plan until we flew up to Norway, after the cruise. We had been to Norway once before and had wanted to return to admire the beautiful fjords God has so intricately created for us.

My husband, John, was driving the vehicle we had rented, and we were heading towards Gudvangen to catch our fjord adventure cruise. It was early morning and, in the distance, he noticed a beautiful waterfall and rest stop.

"Would anyone like to stop here?" he asked. We pressed our faces against the windows to see if it was something we should not miss, but we all agreed it was a great place to stop. Because it was early, we were the first car arriving at this location, so we parked in the empty parking lot, grabbed our cameras and set out to hike towards the sound of the falling cascade of water, which we could faintly hear in the distance. As I walked along, enjoying the surrounding beauty, I looked down and I suddenly froze in my footsteps. In the middle of nowhere, obviously left from a group from an earlier tour bus, was a circular sticker stuck to the ground with the number **13**. Once I regained my breath, I motioned to Janet. I'll never forget her words that morning. She said, "You are right where you are supposed to be again, Kate."

It was through these kinds of experiences that I have learned to trust in God and in His grand plan for us. I know some people would call it a coincidence or fate or pass it off as nothing at all, but what I'm telling you is that this is how God speaks to us. When you are perceptive and open in prayer, you become more aware of His presence and in tune with the purpose for your life.

If you can believe in a near-death experience, then why can you not believe in miracles and angelic interventions, if for nothing more than to nourish your soul and make you a better and kinder person? As we all know, Jesus cured the sick, fed the multitudes and raised people from the dead, but even our smallest and most inconsequential acts of kindness are mighty works in the sight of God. How do you know your prayers haven't saved someone's life?

A few weeks before leaving for the Baltic, at the end of Mass on Sunday, our priest announced the next gift God had in store for us. His words still penetrate my heart. He announced, "The trip to Israel is now a go. We have enough interested pilgrims, but there are still a few openings left if anyone is interested."

I looked over at John and with a distinct whimper in my voice said, "That is really where I wanted to go." For I knew that is where the Gospel was born and was launched to the ends of the Earth. How blessed could one be to experience the place where it all began? The very thought overwhelmed my soul.

The trouble was that we had now already depleted our vacation days and our budget for travelling for the year, and we both felt this calling was nothing we could consider at the time. We were feeling extremely blessed and fortunate that our health, particularly mine, had started to allow us to move forward with our lives by sharing new adventures together abroad, but we still had to pick our battles.

The next Friday, on the way to work, John said to me, "Why don't you call the parish office and get some information on the Israel trip?" I listened in disbelief, but he warned it was for information purposes only. He said, "Don't get your hopes up now, but I'll admit I'm curious. Find out when they are going, how much it will cost and how many seats are left." I got to my computer and sent an e-mail off to the secretary of our parish. As I buried myself in my work, I waited patiently to see the reply e-mail appear on my screen.

Once I received the details on the pilgrimage to the Holy Land, our plan seemed to develop and fall into place.

The next day, we placed a call to the woman who was organizing the trip with the tour company. She said she "had two seats left for Israel" and they were ours if we wanted them! The rest was meant to be.

That summer passed quickly. A couple of weeks before we were scheduled to leave for Israel, the health of John's mother, Nancy, worsened at the nursing home.

She was 97 years of age, and they had now classified her condition as palliative care. You know once they move the coffee cart into your room permanently, it isn't a good sign. She had been alone since John's dad passed away three years before at the age of 94. She was now lying in her bed instead of sitting in her chair.

John drove to Toronto four times in the last week to accompany his sisters, each time thinking 'this will be the last.' John said it was "hard to leave her" and something kept "drawing him back in." Nancy, being still in sound mind, insisted we continue to take our planned trip to Israel.

One day, she even seemed to rally, and on that day, she asked John if he had ever dreamed of his father. John felt sad saying he had not. His mother told him she had dreamt of Frank that night, and he was holding his hand out, telling her it was okay, he was waiting for her to join him in Heaven. When John told me of this dream, I immediately said to him that I did not believe it was a dream. I told John that I believed it was a sign or another vision—her vision.

The evening before we left Israel, we both visited his mother. I had been blessed, three years before, to be the last person in the family to speak with John's dad, so I knew the importance of this visit, which I thought could be our last. As I walked into her room, I immediately made a U-turn and walked back out before she saw me. It was in that hallway I cried and regained my strength enough to re-enter the room and centre my attention on this woman, whom I had always admired from the first day I had met her.

That evening, my admiration was magnified, and her pain consumed me. As soon as Nancy looked into my eyes, she told me, "It wasn't a dream," and as I held her hand, I reassured her that I also believed it wasn't either. I remember thinking that no suffering is greater than to live without God's love. As I searched for the silver lining, I could see this was coming from a woman who had taken more pride in possessions and was not particularly religious throughout her lifetime. Since moving to the nursing home, Nancy had voiced her own pain, suffering and loneliness to others, but she grew in huge strides in her later years, expressing concern and caring for others. She telephoned me during every round of my chemotherapy and talked to me with gentle, kind and loving compassion.

I'm a strong believer that people come into your life for a reason. I feel great respect, wonder and admiration for John's parents, who were placed in my life to teach me how to be a good grandparent and how to grow old graciously. They loved to hear about our worldly adventures and were engaged in our stories, as they no longer could travel. They accepted each phase of their lives gallantly, and they placed their memories—and their children—above all their possessions.

On November 1, 2012, we left for Israel for 13 days, to arrive back on November 13, which, incidentally, marked the three-year anniversary date since it was announced I had breast cancer. You say, "more coincidences?" I say, "what are the chances?"

My father drove us to and from the meeting place of our group. When I bid him goodbye, I hugged him tightly and wished he and my mother were coming with us. It was a trip they should have done years earlier when their health was stable, but I could see in his eyes that he was thrilled we were making the journey to this wonderful country which was so full of spirituality, so small in size, yet so important to us all.

We were warned that there would be strict security inspections from El Al airline before the normal airport security inspections for all passengers flying into Tel Aviv. Our eyes fixated on the number of armed guards and dogs who stood off to one side of the roped lines. I had to remind myself we were still in Pearson International Airport in Toronto, in our free and beloved country. We all watched as each person was approached, questioned and interviewed.

My husband noticed the gate numbers overhead. I did, too, but I didn't say anything to him. They were numbered as Gate 511 through 517. John finally looked into my face and asked me the question I had been anticipating since we arrived at this location. "What do you think the chances are we get Gate 513?" he asked me. My eyes looked up at the gate numbers again before they returned to focus on his face.

"Pretty darn good, I would say."

"Well, that would be 1 in 7 chances, which, in the odds of probability, are pretty unlikely if my calculations serve me correctly," John replied.

We inched forward in the line, and we spoke nothing more about the gate numbers. We were more nervous about the tension in the line than anything else at the time.

We finally arrived at the front of the line to be interviewed. They began questioning us about the contents of our bags, our intentions and the purpose of our trip. They seemed to be more interested in who we were travelling with and when we planned to return. The officials wrote notes on clipboards and started placing stickers on our passports, and then they directed us over to the next official to our left.

145

As we stood there waiting for our next instructions, a woman announced our next move. She said, "Gate 513, please."

It was then my inner self started to chatter: "One in seven chances, eh? I told you. It's not insane anymore. I tell you, I can feel it, I'm right where I'm supposed to be, and this gate is telling me I'm supposed to go to Israel."

John smiled over at me as we entered the gate. These signs came to me for the same reason we were lucky enough to get the last two tickets for this trip, I thought.

The tension I had been feeling dissipated, and complete calmness came over me. I was no longer worried about entering a war-torn country, one that was always in news headlines that convinced most travelers not to visit. Jesus was with me; I could feel Him. I entered Israel with the feeling what would happen was meant to happen, and so be it if I was there. I knew I was right where Jesus wanted me to be.

Those 13 days were indescribable. The weather for November was above seasonal temperatures, and the locations we visited were unlike any other travel location we had ever seen. There were 40 of us accompanied by two priests and one passionate and knowledgeable tour guide, who had been there 35 times. We also had a local travel guide who had lived there all his life, spoke Hebrew and knew the brutal daily realities of the Middle East politics. Besides God, he was also there to protect us.

We took in all the sites most tourists want to cover in the Holy Land. We visited Caesarea, Nazareth, Galilee, Capernaum, the Primacy, Beatitudes, the River Jordan, Cana, Mount Tabor, Beit Shean, Jerusalem, the Mount of Olives, the Via Dolorosa, the Holy Sepulchre, the Western Wall, Qumran, Bethlehem, Shepherd's Field, Yad Vashem, Mount Zion, the Upper Room, the Dormition, and the world's lowest point on earth, the Dead Sea. We celebrated

Masses in the Basilica of the Annunciation, at the site of the Transfiguration of the Lord, at the Church of the Holy Sepulchre with our Mass of the Resurrection, at Shepherds' Field and at the church of the Last Supper.

It would be hard to select a favourite day while we were in Israel, since every day was special. The two most moving moments for me were our baptismal recommitment in the River Jordan and our marriage recommitment vows in Cana, the site where Jesus's first miracle took place at a wedding. Both of these sacramental experiences were remarkable, miraculous and momentous for me. The celebration of these two sacraments felt very much like they felt the first time, but what we felt here was much deeper. It made me feel blessed and forgiven and like I had been given a second chance at life!

I've always struggled with the idea of the River Jordan's water baptizing Jesus, but knowing Jesus walked and immersed Himself into that river made me feel like this was the holiest of waters in the whole world. I believe it was Jesus's body and the Holy Spirit itself that made the whole river sacred. What we must understand is that Jesus could have stayed and ruled forever on the Earth. But that was not the Father's plan. The sending of the Holy Spirit was the fulfillment of God's plan.

Our immense hope, at baptism, gives us the ability to die with Him and be reborn on the last day in a similar fashion to Christ, who was raised up. Think about it. What a way to finish the final chapter of our lives!

The other profound experience for me happened at the Western Wall, also known as the Wailing Wall. I'll never forget this experience for as long as I live. It was on November 8, 2012.

Our pilgrimage tour took us to the Holy Sepulchre for a 9:00 a.m. Mass. Our group arrived at the Western Wall at 1:00 p.m., at which time we divided up into two groups—men and women. The men lined up to pick up their yarmulkes, and the women started to write their prayers on notepads in preparation to place them into the cracks of the wall, as millions of other pilgrims had done before us. I then joined a few other women, and we took turns taking our tourist photos of each other. That is when the mood changed, and we became serious. We each approached the Wall and took in our prayer time.

The first time I approached the Wall, I closed my eyes and put my left hand on the wall, resting my forearm up to my elbow against the wall. I leaned in close with my face to the wall. The left side of my body had always been my weakest due to illness, so this position seemed to be fitting.

Normally, when you close your eyes, you see darkness, especially when you are leaning toward a shaded structure. As I prayed, I could hardly concentrate, as I could see flashes of light going past my eyes unlike anything I had ever seen before. I felt an incredible strength. I can't explain it other than that I felt I was experiencing God's love and light, which is the only safeguard against evil and eternal darkness.

Strength is something I have always prayed for God to give me. Maybe it took going to Israel to earn that strength. The first time, although my eyes were tightly closed, I saw white flashing lights as I prayed with my left hand and arm on the wall. I remembered Matthew 18:20: "For where two or three are gathered together in my name, there am I in the midst of them."

Communal prayer is powerful, and I know that when we gather together to pray as a community, the presence of Jesus is brought to us in a special way. I could truly feel the power and the strength of our prayers in this holy place where crowds gather in prayer.

As I backed away, I knew immediately I had to retrace my footsteps to this Wall again, as something seemed to be calling me. I sensed the distinguished and enormous power of prayer here. After waiting for a free spot on the wall once again, I closed my eyes, and this time, I placed both hands on the wall and leaned into the wall. I swear, this time I could feel the wall vibrating. It was another new experience I had never imagined or expected. I found this place so alluring and captivating. I started to pray for my family and my children. Then I turned my prayer towards John's mother, Nancy, whom we had left back in Canada, nearing the end days of her life.

I have never made it a practice to ask God to take some-one's life or end their pain and suffering, and I wasn't about to start. I guess I figured that was God's job. I only asked God, as I always did, to "listen to her heart." I told God that I already knew and believed God's sign that Frank was waiting in Heaven for her, as she'd told us the day before we left for Israel. I told God she was tired and she was ready, that she wanted to be with Him and Frank again.

As I closed my prayers and backed away from the wall, my friend was waiting for me, but I could barely see her because the tears were flooding from my eyes. She grabbed me and hugged me and asked me if I was okay. She then told me my husband was worried about me, as the group had gathered and I wasn't back yet. We hugged each other as we walked in the direction of our group.

As we walked out of the Old City, back to our hotel, I felt emotionally drained and exhausted. When we arrived back to our hotel in Jerusalem, I took the elevator up to our room to freshen up. John stayed in the lobby, where he could access the Wi-Fi Internet connection. Every day since we embarked on our journey, he had checked for an update on his mother from his sisters in Canada. We had heard updates for four continuous days, and after that, the last four days brought no news.

As John appeared in our room, he looked at me with sorrow-filled eyes and said, "Kate, Mom passed away today."

I hugged him, and as soon as I could regain my breath, I asked him, "What time today?"

He said, "11:30 a.m. Canada time [5:30 p.m. Israel time]." Immediately, I did the calculation in my head, and it turned out my mother-in-law had gone to be with God four and a half hours after I had prayed and talked to God about her at the Wall. I truly believe God listened to her heart and heard my prayers in this most holy place. She finally received her wish and joined her beloved Frank to live together in Heaven with Jesus. My prayer was answered that day, God bless her. Shalom. Peace.

I truly believe everyone should go to the Holy Land at least once in their lifetime. Most of the people who tell you not to go have never been and likely have got their information from the evening news. Anyone who has gone there will tell you to go. A pilgrimage is truly a journey where you "go with God with the intent to grow your faith." The purpose of a pilgrimage is to arrive at a more profound relationship with God. Don't go thinking you are going to pray all the time, either, for that would be called a retreat.

A successful pilgrimage will infinitely change you and put you in a different spiritual place in your life. It puts you in a place where nothing is the same for you anymore when you hear Scripture, see pictures or watch movies. My pilgrimage to Israel gave me new meaning and every place became real. It's truly unimaginable, and my experience was certainly nothing I had ever anticipated when I first said, "That's where I want to go."

One last miracle worth noting also happened during this trip. We left Israel for home on November 13, 2012. On the brochure we were given were Scripture passages for each day we were there. On the 13th, our Scripture reading was from Matthew 28:20: "I am with you always."

Within 24 hours after our return home, on Wednesday, November 14, 2012, Hamas, the Islamist group that controls the Gaza Strip, claimed responsibility for firing rockets at Jerusalem and Tel Aviv. Our leaving on November 13 was again confirmation that I felt Jesus was leading me through the fire and placing me back where I was supposed to be yet again. Sirens sounded in Jerusalem for the first time since they had been struck by Palestinian rockets in 1970. "As the mountains surround Jerusalem, so the Lord surrounds His people both now and forevermore. The scepter of the wicked will not remain over the land allotted to the righteous . . . Peace be upon Israel" (Psalm 125).

Back at home, on November 14, I drove to the grocery store. I was searching for a product my parents had asked me to get for them. I was still off from work for the day, catching up on unpacking, laundry and recovering from jetlag, so I decided to run this small errand for them. I didn't shop regularly in this particular store, so I looked up and down all the aisles. Tired and frustrated, I didn't want to waste any more time wandering around, so I asked the clerk what aisle the item would be found in. I wasn't surprised and my ears almost rang when he said, "Aisle 13, Madam." Again, I walked away saying, "Of course, where else would it be today?" After all, I'm back where I am supposed to be.

The coincidences kept coming. Even simple twists of fates, the kind that anyone would normally simply brush off or not pay any attention to, I now was unable to ignore. On November 23, John and I decided to go on a date night and view a new movie. He ordered the seats online, and the machine then assigns you the "next best available seats." We got to the show, and as we are walking in, he took out the tickets. We were in row J or K, seats number 13 and 14. Could this mean John and Kate, 13 and 14? How can this keep happening! Well, I believe that even in the simplest circumstances, God is always with us.

Three months after my father's death, I had an appointment for a test in the Nuclear Medicine Department at the same hospital where my father had passed away. As I neared the hospital, I looked at the instructions for the location—Building B, Level 2. My appointment was only down the hallway from where my father had taken his last breath. As I repeated the steps and became reacquainted with the same hallway, my stomach started to churn. I could feel my breathing start to change. Memories started flooding back to me from that last day. As I placed my purse and clothing into the locker, I noticed the number on the lock in my hand. The only one available was Number **13**. I whispered to myself, "Yes, Kate, you are going to be okay."

My dad used to tell me that he knelt down every night beside his bed and prayed for me before turning in. I now had my own angel, this time standing with God watching over me.

Chapter 12
Animals Can Be Angels, Too

*In a loud voice they sang: "Worthy is the Lamb,
who was slain, to receive power and wealth and
wisdom and strength and honor and glory and
praise!" Then I heard every creature in Heaven
and on Earth and under the Earth and on the
sea, and all that is in them, singing: "To Him who
sits on the throne and to the Lamb be praise and
honor and glory and power, for ever and ever!"*

—Revelation 5:12–13

It seems eccentric—and is highly embarrassing for me—
to devote a whole chapter to a pet, but because of "the
warning," Nike became part of a mystery. I can only think it
is because the Earth is home to between 10 and 14 million
species of life in the animal kingdom, and we should
never forget that they all have extraordinary purposes and
reasons to be here. Pets, in general, have closer ties with
man, and for that reason, we can see their remarkable abilities here on Earth. Until you have loved an animal, part
of your soul remains unawakened, and you never know

the true meaning of "best friend" until you bond with a furry friend.

I've had numerous special pets in my lifetime, but my last cat, Nike, was one of the most significant animal-related blessings in all of my life. Those of you who have owned a pet will understand the bond between a human and the precious animals we love. An animal's loyalty is unfaltering. A pet doesn't judge and doesn't care what mood you are in or how you look; he or she loves you unconditionally. We all yearn for this kind of love, and we can learn from them as well.

Nike came to me as a rescue animal. A former neighbour had found her pregnant and homeless. The neighbour let her have her three adorable kittens, for whom Nike made the most exquisite mother. Between my neighbour and Nike, her kittens received the finest possible start to life.

When it was time, we found homes for the kittens, and I adopted Nike. I named her Nike because she had the Nike swoosh directly under her chin. As told to me later, by my editor, Nike was the name of a Greek goddess. She said "You named your cat – the angel who would help you through your cancer treatment – after the winged goddess of victory!" Between that and Nike's catch phrase, "Just Do It," I believe her name was precisely appropriate!

Pets quickly become a part of our families. When a beloved pet passes away, a huge void is left in your family and in your heart. The words we use to reflect the intensity of their loss—"searing," "tormenting," "wrenching," "ripping me apart" or "my heart is breaking." It's understandably upsetting when you are grieving and people say to you, "It was just a cat, for heaven's sake" or "It was only a dog." "So when are you going to get another one?" These people are ignorant of the pure love emanating from these uncomplicated God-given creations to which we bond. I've often thought, perhaps that is why *DOG* spelled backwards spells *GOD*.

The degree of hurt and anger that comes from uncaring or misguided statements, results in feelings that are misunderstood and invalidated. Such tactlessness and insensitivity have even been known to damage or end relationships.

Animals and humans are different creations, each serving God in their own special way. Animals are an aid to mankind. They don't have to learn anything except in the wild kingdom—survival. On the other hand, the purpose of a pet is to love mankind and to teach and show us how to love. In my world, Nike never left my side, especially during my cancer journey. She had the most human-like personality of any pet I've ever known. Her soul was pure, with no agenda except to be with me as my animal-friend companion and partner along my road in life.

The white wing-like marking around her neck stretched over the right side of her back. I always called it her angel wing, and in the ugliest and scariest moments of my journey, she loved me unconditionally and brought me back to reality. She was my devoted and loving best friend, whom I always said was an angel who came to me. She needed me, and I needed her. Often I would say to her, "Are you my angel?" and she would look at me, and her eyes would absorb my words like two sponges. When I lost her, I felt the deepest grief ever. Animals provide such an unconditional love. They take it, and they give back tenfold.

She gave me agape love. If you look at the definition for *agape* love, it means selfless, sacrificial, unconditional love, the highest of the four types of love in the Bible. This Greek word and variations of it are found throughout the New Testament. Agape perfectly describes the kind of love Jesus Christ has for His Father and for His followers. How interesting my little Greek goddess taught me the true definition of this Greek word!

The tradition of agape, or unconditional love, is not exclusive to any one religion. Actually, it is a major underlying principle found in religions worldwide. The concept of altruistic love is one that challenges the spiritual person to "love your enemies" or to "love without thought of return." It is a love that flows out to others in the form of kindness, tenderness, charitable giving and compassion.

Compassion is the feeling of empathy for others. It is the emotion we feel in response to the suffering of others that motivates a desire to help. Acting in accordance with one's self-concept is critical for the expression of care and compassion. Ranked a great virtue in numerous philosophies, compassion is considered in almost all the major religious traditions as among the greatest of virtues.

On October 16, 2012, two months to the day, prior to losing my perfect angel, I had yet another "dream." This was the first time my dream involved flying. I dreamt I had already been in Israel, and I came back and was standing in a bathroom. My mother had come over to look after Nike, which she was in fact planning to do for our impending trip.

In my dream, my mother presumed I had not left for my trip yet, but I'd told her I had left, and I had come back to make sure she was there to take care of my cat. I told her I had been in Israel already, and I was in a car being escorted around Israel, but I had to come back to check them and to tell her that I loved them. All of a sudden, I floated upward. Mom looked up and threw me a kiss, and I disappeared back to, I presume, the place I'd said I had been.

I viewed this at the time as a dream, not a vision, but now I have to wonder. This has never happened before or since, but as Peter Pan said, "The moment where you doubt whether you can fly, you cease from ever being able to do it."

Two mornings after this dream, on October 18, 2012, when I arose at 6:00 a.m. to feed Nike—it was now two weeks before we left for Israel—I heard a blood drop hit the kitchen floor. Then another drop of blood and then an another. I looked down and saw blood running down the top of my left leg, but when I cleaned it off, there was no cut. Another strange sign, I thought.

Every morning, Nike would make a special sound, and as I stepped out of the shower, there would always be a toy for me to throw so I could play catch with her. If she couldn't find me, she would let out a meow and call me. John said she was such a needy cat, but I'm almost convinced it was me that made her that way.

We had only been in our home two months when we adopted her into our family, and she was with me for eight years, by my side, all the time, watching my every movement when I was home. She and I had a routine in the morning and at night; leaving a giant hole in my home and in my heart, the day I lost her.

She was such a happy and social soul. She lived life with gratitude yet was totally there just for me. She acted much like a dog playing fetch, greeting us at the door, sitting under the dinner table when we had dinner, and sleeping on our bed. At night, I would get up and go to the bathroom, and she would follow me, lie down by my feet, and give me those love bites cats do. She showed me so much affection in so many ways. For a long time, upon entering the house, with tearful eyes I still saw her everywhere.

Under the Christmas tree and in front of the fireplace were her happy, warm places. She loved blankets and I couldn't lie down without her jumping up on me.

That's what always intrigues me about animals. As people, we think we can decide to be happy, but you can't decide to be happier any more than you can decide to be taller. You can summon a happier life by developing the most important qualities of happiness, but then it is all up to you. Appreciation is the purest, strongest form of love. It is the outward-bound kind of love that asks for nothing and gives everything. It goes hand in hand with unconditional love—that's what animals teach us every day.

Because she was a rescue animal, we were never sure if her stomach problems were because someone had kicked her or treated her badly. She also had asthma. While John and I were in Italy for three weeks to celebrate our 25th wedding anniversary, my dad came over twice a day to feed Nike and to keep her company. Dad would come to our home and read a book and would stay for two two-hour intervals each day just to pet her and keep her company. When we flew to the Baltics and to Israel, my mother came and slept at our house to be with Nike so she wouldn't be alone. Nike loved people, and she loved the companionship. Even though I enjoyed travelling, I always struggled with leaving and being away from this beautiful, precious soul. Now I suffer her absence.

It was when she started eating less that I became worried, although her personality never changed. She would still greet us and want to play, and she would follow me around every minute. It was then I blessed her with the holy water I had brought home with me from Israel. Some may cringe at that thought and say it is sacrilegious, but I believe every life has a soul, and that soul knew love better than some people I've known on this Earth.

By the end, she had lost two and a half pounds in six weeks, and her breathing became rapid. Her rhinestone collar hung sadly around her neck. She was suffering so badly. It was then I made one of the hardest decisions of my entire life. I knew there was only one recourse and as the steward of this precious gift God had entrusted to our care, I was accountable both to Him and to her—His suffering creature.

It was December 16, 2012. I stayed with her to the end, which was so difficult, but I felt I owed it to her to be with her, as she had been so loyal to me. I wanted her to hear and be comforted by my voice.

A purr could no longer be heard. But neither was there any more pain to be endured. My beloved pet had left it all behind, and I was in my promised dark hour.

As Joy Davidman told her husband C. S. Lewis on her deathbed, "The pain now is part of the joy then. That's the deal."

Nike was so special and unique; and I miss her. Her memory will remain with me forever. She came to us a stray but knew nothing but love for eight years. Now I pray she is in Dad's arms and that both will be waiting for me when I cross over to be in God's light. A thought came into my mind. I wondered how many days since Nike died did Dad pass away? I wondered if there was any significant numbers in that equation. Well, it was **123** days! There's that number presenting itself yet again!

And those of you who share in one of these remarkable bonds and have experienced this kind of unconditional love, you will be familiar with this rich landscape of the caring lives of pet guardians.

In dreams, I have seen her. As I draw near to her, she rises up on two legs, and her body transforms into an angel with wings but with human features. I'm reassured that whatever form she is in when we meet again, I will recognize her spirit and the unconditional love she taught me, and I will know it is her. *Angel* is another Greek word, meaning "messenger."

J. P. Moreland, C. S. Lewis and Peter Kreeft—three outstanding Christian apologists—have explored the theological implications of animal immortality and the existence of non-human "souls" within animals. Their words resonate with blinding lucidity.

I believe in the words I once heard a child say when he saw his pet die: "People are born so they can learn how to live a good life—like loving everybody all the time and being nice. Pets already know how to do that, so they don't have to stay as long."

Recently, Pope Francis's audience was devoted to the subject of creation and the new Heaven and Earth. He said, "At the same time, Sacred Scripture teaches us that the fulfillment of this marvelous plan cannot but involve everything that surrounds us and came from the heart and mind of God."

In Romans 8:2, Apostle Paul says it explicitly when he says, "Creation itself will be set free from its bondage to decay and obtain the glorious liberty of the children of God."

Other texts in the Bible (2 Peter 3:**13**; Revelation 21:1) utilize the image of a "new Heaven" and a "new Earth" in the sense that the whole universe will be renewed and will be freed, once and for all, from every trace of evil and from death itself. Bringing all things into the fullness of being, of truth and of beauty, is the design that God—the Father, Son and Holy Spirit—willed from eternity.

While grieving my pet, a dear friend sent me "The Rainbow Bridge." I found this poem brought me a huge amount of comfort in my time of loss. I understand there are several versions of this poem circulating, the original version being written by William N. Britton. This is the version a dear friend sent to me. May it offer the nurturing supportive hug that we all need when we experience the loss of a kindred spirit and help us cope with the vast mystery of what happens to our pets.

The Rainbow Bridge

Just this side of Heaven is a place called Rainbow Bridge.

When an animal dies that has been especially close to someone here, that pet goes to Rainbow Bridge. There are meadows and hills for all of our special friends so they can run and play together. There is plenty of food, water and sunshine, and our friends are warm and comfortable.

All the animals that had been ill and old are restored to health and vigor. Those who were hurt or maimed are made whole and strong again, just as we remember them in our dreams of days and times gone by. The animals are happy and content, except for one small thing; they each miss someone special to them, who had to be left behind.

They all run and play together, but the day comes when one suddenly stops and looks into the distance. His bright eyes are intent. His eager body quivers. Suddenly he begins to run from the group, flying over the green grass, his legs carrying him faster and faster.

You have been spotted, and when you and your special friend finally meet, you cling together in joyous reunion, never to be parted again. The happy kisses rain upon your face; your hands again caress the beloved head, and you look once more into the trusting eyes of your pet, so long gone from your life but never absent from your heart.

Then you cross Rainbow Bridge together . . .

—Unknown

Chapter 13

13 Angels: "I Am with You Always"

*Then Jesus came to them and said, "All author-
ity in Heaven and on Earth has been given to me.
Therefore go and make disciples of all nations,
baptizing them in the name of the Father and of
the Son and of the Holy Spirit, and teaching them
to obey everything I have commanded you. And
surely I am with you always, to the very end of
the age."*

Matthew 28:18–20

I've been told our spirit guides, angels or God can guide us through our feelings, thoughts and words through visions and signs. One of the ways they can create our spiritual awareness, or "awakening," is repeating numbers, or number sequences, to ensure we notice and get their messages from God. The coincidences that so commonly occur in our lives are orchestrated by these guides.

Angels do their utmost to get our attention and to communicate with us. In this way, they help us to heal our lives. It's easy to discount the signs they give us, and we usually write them off as mere coincidences or our imagination, but for me, the more I received, the stronger I felt their presence—and with it, a tremendous responsibility.

The scribes and Pharisees wanted to challenge Jesus. They asked for a sign so Jesus could prove His power and authority. What they didn't know was that Jesus didn't have to prove Himself to anyone. People still often take on that same attitude, but God doesn't do things to make us believe, even today. It is when we recognize the amazing things He does and we recognize the signs that we grow in faith.

Some people believe a sequence of 111 indicates your spiritual guides are with you, and at the time, you can change whatever you are thinking; 444 is often perceived as confirmation they are there guiding you, and 555 can be translated to mean some radical change is going to happen.

For me, by now, you may have guessed my repeating number signs are the numbers **13** and **23**. I thought it was number-appropriate to save Chapter **13** for this introduction! I'm guessing my angels hope I see and acknowledge the same numbers are repeating right in front of me, over and over again, throughout my life just so I notice His work and Him.

When it happens, it feels like I'm receiving three-dimensional vibrational-frequency life-lesson messages. The more I have become aware of this, the more it brings me hope, peace and love, as well as a feeling that something quite magical and Divine is taking place in my life and that I'm on my true life path. Love has its own vibrational field. I'm also told if you don't tap into these occurrences and trust in their higher good, there's a very good chance you are missing the Divine thoughts you are being sent.

A rush of **13s** came in once again: 12 disciples and Christ. The God who promised Moses, "I will be with you," in Exodus 3:12, extends the same promise to us through Jesus: "I am with you always, until the end of the age." For me, this made over 25 number **13s** in three and a half years since I was told about my cancer. I read once, "The number **13** promise is always presented in the presence of unfavorable circumstances, though in time, the circumstances will give way to the birth of the promise" (Stephen Gola).

When I received "the warning" vision of my cat (Nike) and my dad passing, it was only three months before my dad's original surgery date of March 22, 2012. Later, it occurred to me that Dad, in fact, was given **13** more months (March 22, 2012 to April 18, 2013). We were told the heart specialist, who was also involved with the vascular surgeon, had hesitated proceeding the year before because Dad had a "sticky heart valve." While further tests were being conducted, Dad told me several times, "I think they really don't want to operate on us old people, as they know we are going to die soon, anyway, so what's the point?"

Dad was frustrated by the whole process, but during this time, Mom and Dad celebrated 65 years of marriage on July 11 of that year. Ten days later, they watched their grandson, who came home from Australia, marry his university sweetheart.

I was one of the lucky ones who were blessed with the luxury of having had a complete relationship with my parents well into adulthood. I was glad "they didn't want to operate on old people"—and what a finale, with two special celebrations and two wonderful days our families were all given to be together. Thank you, God! Cancer has taught me to embrace the gifts in our lives instead of holding on tightly to the disappointments. I'm glad Dad didn't have that operation **13** months before.

Sometime after we lost Dad, I talked in detail with his vascular surgeon. He said Dad had complained about severe chest pain at 6:30 p.m. on April 18, 2013, the day we lost the most remarkable man—not in surgery but seven and a half hours into recovery. He died at 7:06 p.m. (add 7

+ 6 = **13**). And if you take 7:06 and subtract the **23** minutes they did compressions on him, which they told us had happened, that brings you to 6:43 p.m.; these digits add up to **13**. That would mean from 6:30 to 6:43 p.m. was the time he was in severe distress, and during that time, he suffered the actual heart attack; a period of **13** minutes.

My husband drove Mom and Dad to the hospital that morning to get Dad there at 6:15 a.m., as he had to be there for 6:30. That also would mean he was in the hospital for a total of **13** hours. Everything pointed to **13**. I can't help but know the angels were with us as 12 disciples; and Christ did say, "I will never leave you."

Now, when the number **13** presents itself, I translate it to mean "my angel presence is around me," and it brings me inimitable comfort and confidence, as Jesus promised us. What number or repetitive symbol is your angel using to get your attention?

I visited Mom and Dad at their home the night before Dad's surgery. We had an extraordinary conversation. Dad was telling me how deeply touched and emotionally moved, he had been by the power he had felt in the Mass he attended and during his anointment, which followed it. To bring Dad further comfort at the thought of the moment of anesthesia the next day, I mentioned the "Footprints" verse, and we talked about its meaning. I told him how I had thought about it when I was on the operating table during my cancer surgery. I told Dad, "It was then I had asked Him to carry me." As the Anesthetist put me under, I had felt an unusual wave just before everything went black. It felt like a unique peace and Divine love washing over me.

Dad smiled, and he looked at me and said, "I'm not worried." I really believe Dad's spiritual journey was nearing completion, and I felt reassured that when Dad felt the severe heart pain **23** hours after our conversation, it was then he was feeling God's presence and His close-ness, as I know he was asking Jesus to carry him then.

Psalm 34 says, "The Lord is close to the broken-hearted." He is there through difficult times, like a broken relation-ship, the loss of a job, during financial difficulties and at the death of a loved one—when we find ourselves crying, "Where are you, God?" When we need Him the most, we think God is the furthest away, but it is then God is closest to us, and it is then when Jesus carries us.

In my mind, I have relived the pebble chain of events of that day over and over—and the last week over and over, and the last month over and over—many more times than you can even imagine unless you yourself have been there. The strangest thing of all is the times I notice on the clock and how they always seem to add up to **13**. Rarely, do they not add up to number **13**.

It seems if I go to bed and wake up in the night, or after a sleep in times of distress, or even when I look at a hockey time clock, these numbers appear to me at the precise moment I look for them. I started recording them as I see numbers like these: 1:39, 2:29, 2:38, 3:10, 3:19, 3:28, 3:46, 3:55, 4:27, 4:36, 4:54 5:35, 5:44, 5:53, 6:07, 6:16, 6:25, 6:34, 7:06, 7:15, 7:33, 7:42, 10:21, 10:57, 11:29, 11:56, 12:01, 12:19 and 12:55. It wasn't until it started happening to me so frequently that I realized how many number combina-tions can really add up to **13**. There were even a couple **23** sequences, 3:**23** and 9:59. Is this coincidence or by chance? This seemed to be less frequent a year after Dad passed, but the clock sequences still miraculously reappear in my time of need or weakness.

When talking about this with my brother later, he said, "Talking about **13**s, did you ever think that with Dad dying on April 18, it was **13** days to the end of the month?"

This was the nonbeliever starting to make sense of my **13**s. But the only comment I will make about this is that my father always said it amazed him how he was blessed with children who were so black-and-white. By this, I mean one who has no doubts of God (me) and another who has every doubt (my brother). I know this really disturbed my parents tremendously to the point they blamed themselves for "not doing the right things to guide him there," but lambs in herds do wander and stray, and it's generally not the shepherd's fault!

In the process of writing this book, the number sequences continued. I was at my job, one day, when I received a telephone message from my husband. When I listened to the voice mail for the details of the message, the woman's voice told me it was left at 2:29 (2 + 2 + 9 = **13**), and it lasted **23** minutes.

Another time, we attended a Rolling Stones concert in Detroit, Michigan, and it wasn't until days later that I realized the concert we had chosen, out of the 15 cities they attended, was their **13**th concert city. When I realized it, I always say, "Of course! Why wouldn't it be?" All these similar number occurrences feel like "Again, I'm right where I'm supposed to be at that particular time."

As far as the clock numbers, they only convince me to rule out chance, and it brings me back to Dr. Raymond Moody's theory of clock mysteries, for these seemed to last mainly for the one full year after my father's death.

In every part of creation, you can find the fingerprint of God. God's accuracy can be observed throughout by the use of numbers. His careful design is everywhere you look. The numbers of days until eggs hatch, for example, are all divisible by seven, which is the number of days in a week. The eggs of a potato bug hatch in 7 days; a canary, 14 days; a barnyard hen, 21 days; ducks and geese, 28 days; a mallard, 35 days; and the parrot and the ostrich, 42 days.

God's wisdom is also seen in the making of animals. The elephant has four legs, and they all bend forward in the same direction. No other animal is made this way. God planned that this beast would have a huge body, too large to live on two legs, but He gave it four fulcrums so it could rise from the ground easily. The horse rises from the ground on its two front legs first. A cow rises from the ground with its two hind legs first. How wise is the Lord in all His works of creation!

God's wisdom is also revealed in His arrangement of sections and segments, as well as in the number of grains. All grains are found in even numbers on the stalks, and the Lord specified thirty-fold, sixty-fold, and a hundred-fold, which are all even numbers. Each watermelon has an even number of stripes on the rind. Each orange has an even number of segments. Each ear of corn has an even number of rows. Each stalk of wheat has an even number of grains. Every bunch of bananas has on its lowest row an even number of bananas, and each row decreases by one, so that one row has an even number and the next row an odd number.

God has caused the flowers to blossom at certain speci-fied times during the day. Carl Linnaeus, the great bota-nist, once said that if he had a conservatory containing the right kind of soil, moisture and temperature, he could tell the time of day or night by the flowers that were open and those that were closed!

The waves of the sea roll into shore 26 to the minute in all kinds of weather. Do you always think these things are by coincidence? If you have one ounce of faith in our God, I think you will start to realize they are not. Genesis **2:3** is the first time a 2 and a 3 appear together in the Bible talking about the Sabbath: "And God blessed the seventh day and made it Holy, because on it He rested from all the work of creating that He had done."

As science probed, searched, experimented and advanced their understanding of the creation that God, had made, there came a point when men could start to determine how exactly it was our bodies were being manufactured. At a certain point, a code—our DNA, as we say—was discovered, and its mysteries began to be revealed. Many have called it God's fingerprint.

Today, it is fair to say, quite a lot has been learned. It has been discovered that humans have **23** chromosome pairs—**23** chromatids from our mother and **23** from our father—and it is via these that our unique physical characteristics as human individuals are specified. These infinite numbers of **23** carry the language specifying our own individual design.

These blueprints have been made by our Creator! The number **23** is important in the making of babies (chromosomes), and interestingly, it first shows up in the New Testament where the numbers 2 and 3 appear together in Matthew **2:3**; it falls in a section of Scripture that speaks about the birth of the greatest baby of all—a baby named Jesus, Jesus of Nazareth!

A human male's number **23** chromatid, from the father's side, looks somewhat like the letter Y. How coincidental is it that one of the names for God the Father is Yahweh, which starts with a Y; according to Scripture, we were "made in God's image."

A female's **23**rd chromatid, from the father's side, looks more like an X, which also looks somewhat like a cross. Our Lord Jesus was hung on a cross to take away our sin, and sin, we learn in Genesis, first came about through the woman, Eve, who listened to the serpent and ate the forbidden fruit. Because of her, for her sake, Adam ate it too.

Serpents are famous for placing themselves in a coiled position when they are at rest. Isn't it interesting our DNA stores within our cells in a coiled position?

So, the X and the Y and the coil are all present. In reproduction, when the woman's chromosomes and the man's chromosomes meet and align with each other, they attach to each other to form pairs. If it is to be a male, then the **23**rd man chromosome (a Y) attaches to the woman's **23**rd chromosome (the X)—like Yehoshua (Jesus in Hebrew) was attached to the wooden cross upon which He died for our sin, through love and suffering, and we were made worthy through His sacrifice.

The "seed" died so that it could bear fruit through its bride, the newly born Christian Church. The Church is the Kingdom of God on Earth because Jesus is still present today in the Church. And billions have been baptized through and into that Church in the name of Jesus. He was crucified in hope that, as Christ defeated death, we too could share in the same victory on our last day. There is no gain without a measure of pain. Even for Jesus Christ, the cross preceded the crown.

Those who are baptized are born again as new children of God through this "bride," which is the Church, like new physical humans are born from the woman, who is the intended bride of a man. In this way as well as others, marriage and reproduction are holy re-enactments of higher, purer and nobler things.

Consider how deep the concept of procreation seems and how it describes the building of a creature, "man," who is sort of a centerpiece for all of the created world. Consider, also, how God makes so many complex things work together so majestically for each other's continued best interests and the achievement of His Divine purposes. It seems natural to quote the Scripture verse "What has God wrought?" from Numbers **23:23**. There's that number again!

Finally, on a different topic, did you know the Latin alphabet has **23** letters, and the Bible was circulated widely in the Latin tongue?

Also, the Americas have 3 nations in North America, 7 nations in Central America, and **13** nations in South America. That adds up to **23** nations. It is a continental land mass where the majority of the population is Christian—from top to bottom. What does that mean? I am not certain, and maybe it means nothing. But since God is never careless, and since God puts our authorities in place over us, and since God can see the end from the beginning, my guess is that it means something significant. Even scientists have determined that, before the Big Bang, there was nothing, and everyone knows something cannot come from nothing—even the universe.

Chapter 14
Safe in My Arms—
The Shores of Normandy

Many are called but few are chosen.
—Matthew 22:14

It wasn't a dream or a vision. This time, I felt a piercing message. It appeared to me in Normandy in October 2013, six months after my father's death, as we landed on the Normandy Beaches.

Since a child, the subject of war piqued my curiosity as it always seemed to be the forbidden topic. On our honeymoon, John and I had found ourselves at a Canadian War Cemetery in France. Ever since then, we always had a longing to go back to Normandy and see the beaches where the soldiers of America, Britain and Canada came ashore on D-Day in 1944.

The previous couple of weeks, we had travelled through France, Belgium and England, and I thought it would have prepared me for what I was about to see and feel. I was surprisingly unprepared for the emotional wave that enveloped me upon our arrival at Juno and Omaha Beaches.

My father was born in 1929, which if you do the math, would make him too young to enlist and be eligible for WWII. It was another blessing. But I was always interested in and felt a deep compassion for the many souls who lived through and truly experienced the horrors of warfare, particularly the ones who died to liberate France—and the world—from the darkest forces imaginable.

My father-in-law Ed was one of those war survivors who never talked about "the War." Through my in-laws, I heard the fateful story about the time he served in the Navy on the HMCS *Athabaskan,* the "Unlucky Lady."

In the early morning hours of April 29, 1944, this ship sunk during combat with German destroyers in the Bay of Biscay, taking the lives of 128 men from the ship's complement of 256. Of the 128 survivors, more than 80 were captured and taken as POWs by German forces, and Ed was one of those men. He became a prisoner of war after being rescued by German E-Boats.

Years later, one of his children pronounced they "didn't believe in God." That was the one day Ed broke his silence and described his captivity. Angrily, he spoke in an unfamiliar tone and at a volume they had never heard before. "Don't let me ever hear you say you don't believe in God again," he said. "While I was immersed in the frigid waters of the English Channel, when the *Athabaskan* sunk, I clung to floats, barely holding on while trying to hold on to other burned comrades."

With tears in his eyes, he continued. "Due to hypothermia and drowsiness, men were screaming as they let go due to the elements, making it impossible for them to hang on any longer. Fear and death surrounded me. It was in all that chaos that I felt the ultimate presence of God, and I just knew I was going to survive and live."

Ed went on to marry and have five children and eight grandchildren. He was a kind and gentle man of few words, but unfortunately, for years, I know he fought personal demons we would today call PTSD (post-traumatic stress disorder).

I thought of this story as I stood at the top of the bluff, where the Omaha Beach Memorial and Cemetery was located. We were awestruck by the 9,000 young American men—and boys—buried there, whose stories were likely just as horrific or worse. As I looked down to the beach, I said to my husband, "I'm going down there. If they fought their way up, I'm going down."

My husband and I said no words as we made our way to what was a lot higher grade than I had imagined. With each step, my mind flashed back to those opening scenes in *Saving Private Ryan*. I kept imagining what the American soldiers thought and felt as they hit this beach and tried to climb up this same grade, fully dressed, loaded with gear and under intense enemy fire.

Then I thought about the soldiers who didn't get the chance to escape the water, and the ones who lay helplessly upon the beach, taking their last breaths. My eyes focused on a concrete German pillbox, which no doubt had contained machine guns that killed a lot of the young soldiers who landed on this beach. It seemed like 30 minutes that day for me, but it was actually three hours that I spent in deep thoughts of meditation, reflection and prayer for those who sacrificed their lives and gave their all for us. The young lives who were lost there are now, forever frozen in time. It is because of their heroism that we enjoy freedom today. It was at these locations that the high cost of sacrifice could fill an ocean with tears.

Along with the overwhelming emotional experience of this day, without an Earthly explanation, I felt the most compelling need to pray the "Our Father" prayer while quietly walking down the hill to Omaha Beach. As we walked onto this deep, vast, uninhabited, sandy beach at low tide, we could hear the waves and the wind. As far as you could see, there was a red sandy beach surrounded by tall grasses. As I stood there, I wondered if the red sand had been permanently dyed by the enormous amount of bloodshed. I can't explain it, but it was at this point I felt not a voice but a "deep-pitted message."

At the time, I assumed it was my intuition, or a deep spirit within me, that said, "Many are called, but few are chosen* . . . they are safe in my arms."

As I turned to go back, ascending the hill, I could taste the sea salt and sand on my lips. Memories flooded into my mind from my childhood days. I thought about the strong wind which had taken hold of me in my one vision. I thought of my papa, Mr. Edwards and Steve, our old neighbor who only had one arm and why they all never talked about these places. I remembered, as a child, asking my mother about the psychiatric hospital we used to drive by, the one that was at one time full of veterans. The cell-block structured building was seven stories in height and had wired mesh sunrooms which were placed at the two ends of each wing on each floor. The men sat on Adirondack chairs on sunny days, staring outwardly, blinded.

The memories I recall, along with my father's words, made me understand why, in war, no one wins. As Dad used to say, "There is death, and then there are worse things than death."

> * *"Called, chosen and faithful"*: The eternal God desires that those who are called out of this world be His chosen ones as well.
>
> This particular phrase was used by Jesus after He spoke a parable in which someone was invited to a wedding but did not have on a wedding garment (Matthew 22:11–14). The lesson of the parable is that when someone is called by God,

that person has a responsibility to respond to the calling and make spiritual changes in his or her life.

The man in the parable who was invited to the wedding had a duty to come dressed for the occasion, which symbolically meant that he was to put on righteousness, but he didn't do that. So Jesus made the famous statement that "many are called, but few are chosen." Therefore, the called-out ones must be spiritually prepared and be clothed with righteousness. For us, parables are used to provoke and challenge us in our everyday lives.

May we forever be thankful and remember all those amazing men and women who so bravely and courageously placed themselves in harms way and offered their lives for the peace and freedom we have today. May we be grateful to those who continue to offer their lives in service to protect us and to sustain peace and justice throughout the world. If only we would realize we are all brothers and sisters in Christ and put an end to war, violence and injustice and live in peace.

Remember the significance of the poppy. (Women should wear their poppy on their right side). The red represents the blood of all those who gave their lives. The black represents the mourning of those who didn't have their loved ones return home. The green leaf represents the grass and crops growing and a future of prosperity after the war destroyed so much. Position the leaf at 11 o'clock to represent the eleventh hour of the eleventh day of the eleventh month, the time that World War I formally ended.

Chapter 15
The Lead-Up

Brothers and sisters: Since we are justified by
faith, we have peace with God through our Lord
Jesus Christ, through whom we have obtained
access to this grace in which we stand; and we
boast in our hope of sharing the glory of God.
And not only that, but we also boast in our
sufferings, knowing that suffering produces
endurance, and endurance produces character,
and character produces hope, and hope does
not disappoint us, because God's love has been
poured into our hearts through the Holy Spirit
that has been given to us.

—Romans 5:1–5

While I was in chemotherapy treatment, our parish started Scripture Study classes. Six months before our Israel trip, I started a five-week "Pilgrim People" Scripture Study group. Pilgrim People was a journey through Scripture which examined how the call of God led the faithful, in both Old and New Testaments, to regard themselves as pilgrims.

God's call sometimes "leads" and sometimes "sends," and the destination can be new, and wondrous, or even dark and dangerous. But it is not the destination that transforms biblical journeys into pilgrimages. Instead, not unlike it was for people in Scripture, our footsteps are set in the right direction when we discover that God is our companion on the journey.

All major landmarks of salvation history were covered in the study program, which also discussed insightful research as well as lively reflections on the contemporary call to every Christian to follow God as a faithful pilgrim. The study began with a discussion of an inspiring line of biblical ancestors who envisioned their lives as pilgrimages, starting with the *Call of Abraham and Sarah* and concluding with Jesus's call to *Come, Follow Me*. This study showed how journeying with this perspective offers our lives direction, purpose and deep meaning.

Once I returned to work, I started to spend a lot of time praying in the park as I walked to and from work. I found the beauty and serenity of this quiet time inspiring. It was the perfect time to talk to God. Quiet time can also give you time to reflect on your life.

Harnessing the power by way of prayer and quieting your mind from everyday chatter helps you connect with your innermost intuition and the beams of light which provide hope, healing and help. During these personal moments, God and I have had some pretty good discussions. As I said, earlier in my life, I had found myself praying less, but now I find myself praying anywhere and everywhere. I don't say that to mean that is all I do, as I live my life like any normal person, only I now have a life where God and I have an active relationship with each other.

A month after my incident in the Basilica, and two months before my life threatening health scare, I found myself on a trip to California. We visited the Mission

San Juan Capistrano. Off to the side of the Serra Chapel (labeled the number **13** point of interest, of course!) was the St. Peregrine's Chapel. It was glowing with candles, and the room was stuffy from the heat of their flames.

For those of you who aren't familiar with this saint, he is the patron saint of cancer sufferers; at the age of 30, he gave his life to God. He joined the Service Order and dedicated his life to caring for the sick, poor and marginalized. At age 60, Peregrine was diagnosed with cancer in his leg. The night before his leg was to be amputated, he dragged himself before the crucifix and begged the crucified Lord to heal him. Falling into a deep, trance-like sleep, he saw Jesus lean down from the cross to touch his leg. He awoke the following morning to find his sores completely healed and his cancer cured.

Being a cancer survivor myself, I knew this story well. What I didn't know was what was going to happen to me in this place. As I went to step up onto the step to enter the warm, glowing chapel, I fell upon my knees in the doorway. I felt that same force as I had the day I passed out in the park. It was like someone pulled me down, only this time I was fully conscious. It was there, on that step, that I began to worship that Super-Being called God—that Someone who controls the universe. I thanked Him for my own personal recovery, and then I pulled myself up, proceeding further into the chapel, where I left all my prayers for everyone I knew who was struggling with this wretched illness.

For me, returning to prayer began when I started asking God, "What is my purpose?" Why did He take the demons from me and save me? Since then, I truly felt reborn, and I've prayed many times, asking Him to help me make sense of what He did for me and to allow me to do His work. I already know God the Creator made me unique—a one-of-a-kind, never-to-be-repeated Divine masterpiece unlike

179

anyone else on this Earth—so now it was up to me to live and breathe my purpose!

After arriving home from this vacation, I received an e-mail from a friend who was alone, telling me she had just found out she had been diagnosed with uterine cancer. She had only told her daughter and her sisters but wanted to tell me, too, knowing I had once been in her shoes and could give her some beneficial advice.

I called her immediately, and we talked and cried together briefly. But a couple of days later, I knew she could use a hug, so I picked up some flowers and drove to her house. She had not been feeling well that day, so when she did not answer, I became concerned but decided to leave the flowers in the doorway.

This was her e-mail:

> The flowers have been saved, and they are absolutely gorgeous. I burst into tears when I opened the front door and out they fell. Then I opened them up, and was putting them into a vase of water, and I burst into tears yet again. Kate, the flowers were gorgeous, and in them, was a sweet decoration of an orange butterfly. I don't know if I told you, but after my dear Daddy passed away, it seemed wherever I went, I saw the real orange butterflies everywhere. In fact, I have a story to compose about them, and how often I saw them in my yard, that I have yet to do. So, the orange butterfly means SO much to me, and there it was in the bouquet from you. It was a sign that my dear Dad is looking out for me. I wanted to share that with you...I know you would smile. Dad is working through you, my dearest friend.

I hadn't known the significance of the monarch butterfly when I'd asked the florist to put this in my friend's arrangement. I'd like to think she was right!

After this friend's cancer surgery, I called her again to see how she was doing. What I did not know was she had been to the surgeon's office only that day and had received the pathology report saying the cancer was caught at stage one, and radiation was the only recommendation to follow. She was amazed, again, at the impeccable timing of my call, telling me she felt it to be a blessing from God. What a gift, and privilege, bestowed on me.

"You are like an angel," she said. Since then, doctors have discovered a brain tumour in her, and as of this writing, they have not yet determined whether it is malignant or benign, but my prayers, friendship, luminaries and hope continue for this dear friend every day, as I believe her good heart has still a lot to accomplish here in this world, under God's will.

Have you ever wondered why Jesus spoke to His disciples in parables? Jesus did this because it was a simpler way for Him to explain the mysteries of the Kingdom of Heaven that were hard to understand. For parables are stories with a lesson. Unfortunately, we as humans "look but do not see, and hear but do not listen or understand." Sometimes we ourselves are the messengers.

Many times, I ask Him to give me the grace to evangelize in new and creative ways and to tell me what I am supposed to do without the fear and insecurities to hold me back. I ask Him to let me be His modern-day advocate—the simple dove among the wolves. Many spiritual books seemed to fall into my hands, and I believe they were a sign that it was time to share the earnest truth with my own experiences. God wanted me, a simple and seeking soul, to write this book. What better way to touch the lives of so many in a wider audience?

In my visions, God told me I needed to help more people understand the bigger picture by opening their hearts and becoming more aware of His presence. He also wanted me to give hope to other people, including those who are members of the exclusive club called Cancer Survivors, of which I am now one.

Chapter 16
Reaching the Frequency

The world says, "Blessed are those who live it up." But Jesus says, "Blessed are those who mourn." It is only those who are capable of loving who are capable of true mourning. To open one's heart is to begin to live.

—Homily on the Beatitudes

*C*hemo brain is a common term used by cancer survivors to describe thinking and memory problems which can occur after cancer treatment. Chemo brain can also be called *chemo fog, chemotherapy-related cognitive impairment,* or *cognitive dysfunction.*

Though chemo brain is a widely used term, I've been told it can be misleading, as it is unlikely that chemotherapy is the sole cause of concentration and memory problems in cancer survivors.

Despite the many questions, it's clear the memory problems can be a frustrating and debilitating side effect of cancer and its treatment. More research needs to be completed on this subject to understand this condition and how memory problems can affect one's everyday life.

Knowing this condition and having experienced some of its symptoms first hand, I think it seems peculiar I never have had any trouble remembering my visions or picking up on the signs I felt were God-given. In fact, I believe I've been vibrating at a higher level, or frequency, and I am more in tune and aware and perceptive, and that is why I receive these insightful messages I celebrate. I have realized that although we may be small, we are all connected to a very big God who is deserving of big things from us, even if we don't know why. But He knows! Love has a vibrational element that has the ability to make the chemical changes that are the healing agents within us.

The morning before Dad's funeral, I walked outside and knelt down and prayed the sincerest prayer I think I ever prayed in my entire life. On many occasions, even my young granddaughter has asked me, "How do you pray, Nana?"

For those of you who don't know, prayer is basically talking to God in your very own way. Talking to God is the purest form of prayer. You should pray where you can have total concentration and become quiet and serene within yourself. This can be in your home, outdoors or anywhere, but choose a quiet, comfortable, peaceful atmosphere. If you need tools like incense or candles to open your mind and heart to God, use them.

Closing your eyes can help you focus and concentrate, and you can always start by talking to God with sincere words and with earnest feelings. Think of Him as a good friend whom you know you can confide in, sitting beside you. The act of desiring a closeness with God is the very best prayer.

Your prayers must be heartfelt. It is said that a true prayer is asking God to set your life in perfect alignment with His Will. Society seems to teach us to be thoroughly independent and self-reliant, making prayer an impossible fit somehow.

You should realize the chatter within your heart and mind is already your automatic prayer. Prayer should be as natural as breathing, but just keep it positive, because you don't want worry to become your prayer. It's always good to remember to learn to talk to Jesus with gratitude by praising and thanking him for the blessings in your life; don't limit prayer only to requests.

It is okay to pray with expectation, as long as it is in our best interests, because it is God's desire to answer you, but know sometimes the answer may not be what we wanted or in the form of what we expected. The answer, as God knows far better than we do, is "it is what it is."

As Clarence Bauman says, "The purpose of prayer is not to inform God of our needs but to invite Him to rule our lives."

Prayer is a wonderful privilege, opportunity and blessing that God has provided to us, His children.

As for me, our home sits up high on a hill, and on a clear day you can see for miles. One day, I felt like I wanted to be closer to God and with nature and all the beautiful God-given gifts He had created around me.

As I looked upward after saying "amen," the most beautiful rays of sunlight were shining down from the sky. You know the ones—the kind of rays you see when you can actually identify bands stretching from the clouds down to the Earth. That Heavenly sign always takes my breath away and makes me want to stare, taking it all in. I looked up and said, "Praise God. Thank you, God." That was the day I felt I had been shown the master plan of the last **23** years and the goosebumps, chills, or *angel bumps*, as I now like to refer to them, confirmed again it was the marvelous truth.

The day of Dad's funeral, I was feeling extremely exhausted from everything that had transpired over the last few days. I had been up the last couple of nights writing Dad's eulogy, and in the daytime, I was making the funeral plans with my mother, brother and husband.

Everything was prepared, and I needed time for myself. As I came into the bedroom, my bed covers were still as they had been when I had awoken. My husband and brother had been with my mother that morning. I had decided it was likely best to lie back down and try to get some sleep, if my mind would forgive me. And if I couldn't sleep, I could always pray, I thought.

I closed the shutters, climbed into bed and snuggled under the covers. I lay there, alone, gazing up at the ceiling as I felt a tear squeeze its way from the corner of my eye and run down my cheek. I still couldn't believe what had transpired over the last few days. It still didn't seem real, but then I realized I had never been here before to even know how it was supposed to feel.

Many times over the last couple of years, I had thought about writing this book. I always started thinking about a title, and many times, I would play around on the computer and search for spiritual sayings or themes, and nothing struck me. I became frustrated, and I thought I could easily be talked out of writing it.

As I lay there, that morning, I started to pray, and it was then it happened! I thought about how long I had been having visions, **23** years. I then heard the doctor's voice from two days before: "We tried compressions, and every-thing to save his life for **23** minutes . . ." As I lay there, Psalm **23** came into my train of thought. My prayer did not end with an *Amen,* as I quietly and quickly swung my legs over to the side of the bed, walked over to my dresser and picked up my Bible. I started to tremble as I turned the pages. I knew Psalm **23**, but I had to be sure.

As I found Psalm **23**, my eyes froze on the words. It was at that moment that I realized I was being given a task—to be an advocate.

As a young child, I was taught that Psalm **23** was referring to a person's return to God at the time of their own death. As I was grieving the enormous loss of my dad, the man I had loved more than anyone on this Earth, I started to believe Psalm **23** was meant for us who are left behind to grieve.

As we walk through the valley of the shadow of a loved one's death, we suffer sadness, anger, doubt, remorse, guilt and confusion, and this can allow negativity, evil and disbelief to quietly enter our hearts. We need to ask our Heavenly Father to protect our souls in this vulnerable and emotional time and to carry us. The passage inspires and encourages unconditional faith and trust in the Lord. I lay back down and thanked God, but I also told Him I was still listening.

It was only then I saw it: It was a greyish spot, like a speck of dust floating from the centre of the ceiling only about two feet above my face, and this spot kept falling like a waterfall, a firefly, over to the right of me. My eyes followed until it was out of my peripheral vision. I looked up again and again, and each time, another one would float in the same direction.

This kept happening, over and over again. I brushed my hair away, thinking a hair might have been in my line of sight, but I would look to the far left, and again it would appear but again float across my view and head toward the right again. The rebel I am, I couldn't even trick it. I couldn't make it fall in the other direction. For a second, I thought maybe something like a blood vessel had broken behind my pupil, and I had better call the doctor, because I knew I wasn't going crazy. It was then I remembered speaking out loud, and I started to ask God, "Are these angels? Is this You, again, showing me something You want me to see?"

I even asked my dad if he were there. Then I thought, why to the right? Why to the right? I then whispered out loud again, "What does He want me to see?"

I turned and looked, and it came to me: Above the doorway, next to my side of the bed, is a doorway to the en suite bathroom. Above it is the crucifix from Jerusalem that I bought at our parish while I was fighting my cancer. There on the dresser table was my "shrine," as John called it.

My dresser, beside my bed, is covered with special pieces. There were photographs of my parents, of my grandmother Rose and of Nike. There is a vase from my dad's parents' 50th anniversary, cancer pins and angels. There is also a small ornamental cat resembling Nike, and it holds her collar with her name and her bell on it. Two rosaries hang over some photos, as does a photograph of Jesus which was given to me by a lady with whom I found a profound connection, years ago, during a hospital stay. She has long passed now.

Since our visit to Jerusalem, a few more items have been added—a small crucifix and four miniature statues of Jesus, the Virgin Mary and two angels. This is not to be confused with worshiping idols. In this space, I have created a serene place to collect my innermost thoughts, and it provides me with a quiet "me place" to pray. If you can't find one, I say create one!

In the four months after Nike passed, I would always light a candle when I was down, because the light of the candle helped me with my grief. It took the darkness away, and it gave me back the light of her spirit in my times of pain. In the early days after Dad passed, I lit the candle for him.

Above the dresser are two pictures, which I brought home from Jerusalem. One is of the Western Wall, where

I had my profound experience, and the other is of the architecture, which I chose because the artist wrote on it, "Dreaming Jerusalem." I liked it when I found it, because most of my visions have come to me "like a dream." I think, on this particular morning, the angel dust was drawing me toward my "shrine."

In the days when I went to the cancer clinic on a daily basis, John used to comment on the date-countdown calendar that hung by the doors as patients came in. The staff were counting the days that were left till spring. One day, while in chemotherapy, I came up with the same idea to get me through my journey. I made flash cards with all the days and weeks left for my treatment.

When John came in, I hid my paper cutting and writing, because I was embarrassed. But then I told him I needed to do this to get through the weeks and days ahead with all the physical things that were happening to my body.

He looked at me and said, "Whatever you need to do baby, you do it. Don't worry about what everyone else thinks; it's about you right now." As L. Frank Baum, the author of *The Wonderful Wizard of Oz,* said, "The true courage is in facing danger when you are afraid." How we do that is up to us because there will be times when it seems like everything that could possibly go wrong is going wrong. Sometimes you have to go through the worst, to arrive at your best. That's when you might have to get back up again, try again, love again, live again and dream again without the hard lesson hardening your heart for good. Quitting life is not an option! Everything in life is temporary. Every time it rains, it eventually stops. Every time you get hurt, you heal. After every night fall, there is always light. Nothing lasts forever.

So this is how the shrine came into being. I decided not to feel embarrassed about my faith, and I put my hand in His hand and did not look back.

The shrine brings me comfort in those times of despair. I fear the thoughts of people saying, "Oh my God, she has gone religious!" but I don't feel it is that way at all. The bottom line, quite simply, is that it's my special place that I created that fulfills and brings me comfort and peace and connects me with our Lord and Saviour.

It's my quiet place. Everyone should have one.

I believe actual religion, as we know it, was created on Earth, not Heaven. Many years ago, when I first started researching near-death experiences, I had heard that because each of us is at a different level of spiritual development and understanding, there are different churches to fulfil knowledge and those voids.

I don't believe that all the wars and distress that have rocked this Earth because of religion are what God wants or what God has created. He is a good and forgiving God. All peace and power comes from Jesus. God doesn't make mistakes. Yes, there have been some awful people in the world who seemed to make historic mistakes in which others have suffered terribly at their will, but their actions were carried out from their own independent decisions, which were separate from God. Choice is the true voice of the heart.

Apart from visiting "the shrine," I do attend public prayer. It is my belief that choosing a religion should be your own personal choice and should come from the heart. I believe we are all drawn to whatever level of faith we get the most out of, and we do have the ability to change and convert to other religions as our inner self grows.

I know the ability to convert can also apply to Muslims, but from what I understand, they are expected to remain faithful to their Islamic beliefs and their Qur'an for their lifetimes, with the motivation to please Allah. It is written in the Qur'an that if they leave Islam and convert to another religion, the penalty is death (unless they were born Christian, and in that case, it would be tolerated).

Indeed, these are difficult choices, but knowing Jesus was not only a prophet but was the Son of God changes everything. Upon my visit to Turkey, Islam was the only religion I ever encountered that really made me feel out-of-touch and uncomfortable, even though the people were warm and wonderful, and their places of worship were really beautiful. If you open your heart, you can empathize with people and appreciate the beauty in our differences.

Experience tells me going to church doesn't make you a Christian any more than standing in a garage makes you a mechanic, but I know Christ gave the world the Church, as God gave Moses the prophets. The Church is God's messenger to the world, and Christ has given His authority to speak the message of truth. In the time of Moses and the prophets, when people didn't like the message, they wouldn't listen. Today it is no different. Becoming a good Christian, I believe, is entirely up to you, and the possibilities in this world are endless. Amen.

Have you ever read the eight Beatitudes while seeing if any of them are representative of you? Try it sometime. You may find it interesting, and you may learn something when you see yourself in some of them—if not now, at some point in your life. Do you mourn? Are you meek? Do you hunger and thirst for righteousness? Are you "poor in spirit"? The most important lesson you will learn is that you are blessed.

I was fascinated by a statement I once heard from a person who was asked, "Do you believe we are now in the end of times?" I loved this reply, and I knew this would also be my answer to anyone: "I can't be certain and know for sure if this is, in fact, the end of times. But there is one thing I do know for sure, and that is I likely have about 40 more years left of my life, give or take."

I pictured this person around my age. They continued to say, "He, meaning Jesus, is either going to come here, or I am going to go there. This is the reason I need to be ready. Therefore, I don't waste my time debating whether we are in the end of times or not."

What does it matter when? Prepare yourself for His coming. Live as though He were coming today, and you will never fear His coming!

In the Bible, Revelation was written by John, in his own words and with language of that time. This is how he thought best to describe the events: "Remember, therefore, what you have received and heard; obey it, and repent. But if you do not wake up, I will come like a thief and you will not know at what time I will come to you" (Revelation 3:3).

We are not supposed to change God's holy ordinance. The Bible clearly says Jesus will come first to take His Church, in the twinkle of an eye (quickly), and He will meet the Church in the clouds—therefore, no one else other than the Church and the angels will see Him. Then the seven years of tribulations will occur here on Earth, while the Groom and the Bride (Jesus and the Church) are having the wedding supper, or feast of celebration, up in Heaven. After the seven years go by, then Jesus will return along with His Church, and this time "every eye shall see Him." He will set His foot on Mount Olive, which will split in two, and He will triumphantly enter Jerusalem as a King to start His millennium-long reign of peace and justice, here on Earth. And the end of times will end all suffering, crying and pain.

For me, either on the last day, when Jesus emerges from the clouds carrying His cross, or when my work is done here and I am called into Heaven to spend life everlasting in paradise with Him, as He promised us salvation, I will be ready; Heaven is only for those whose hearts are filled with the love of God.

"For the Lord sees not as man sees: man looks on the outward appearance, but the Lord looks on the heart" (1 Samuel 16:7). If only we could do the same! In today's society, we all seem so intrigued by the appearances of good-looking people who dress well and run in the right social circles. God isn't concerned about outward appearances, or age, for that matter. He cares about what's in our hearts for that is how He knows us through the beauty of our soul.

One evening, shortly after my father's passing, I was awakened at 2:00 a.m., and as I walked into the room where we have our computers, I could see the blue power light, but I could also hear a knocking sound. I remember thinking, "Here's that knocking sound again, only this time, it isn't the refrigerator!"

It was at that moment I had an outpouring of ideas and thoughts for chapters in this book, and they came to me so fast that I grabbed a pencil and started scribbling them down, as they were coming into my thought process so quickly. It was like the laptop or someone in the room was telling me it was time to get this down.

Since then, I've heard this called "automatic writing," which is explained as positive energy as part of a Divine intervention that connects us to self-awareness, or self-knowing.

In the last **23** years, this never happened until the day my beloved father died. I have to believe the level of my authentic faith strengthened me through my life experiences, allowing me to expand my awareness to the higher power that was clearly at work. This allowed the spirit within me to awaken and receive their comforting messages through visions.

The next day was the day of Dad's funeral: the **23**rd of April, 2013.

When I am asked about my favorite season, I say spring. Although I was born in the fall and have always loved the rich, beautiful fall colours, I always loved spring best. I have always been mesmerized by everything coming back to life after the long, cold and blustery winter. Spring comes after all the branches looked like twigs and the air was so still except for the cold wind.

In winter, everything appears to be in a frozen state or, worse still, dead with no chance of revival. It's when the sun comes out with the warm whispers of spring that the buds, birds and blossoms seem to come out of nowhere.

I always thank God for this reprieve from the harsh weather and acknowledge His promise of hope and new life. I always felt spring went hand in hand with God's promise at Easter.

On the day of Dad's funeral, John opened the back door and announced that all the daffodils were suddenly in full bloom. John had planted over 100 daffodils bulbs in the autumn so they would appear as a spring surprise for me, as he knew daffodils symbolized "cancer," and he wanted me to feel the healing nature of their refreshing beauty every year thereafter. It was for that reason, and also because the squirrels prefer tulip bulbs over daffodils. Because our home backed onto a forest, it seemed like the wiser choice.

I'll never forget John's words this day: "It is truly the day of resurrection, Kate! Yesterday, none of them were in flower, but today they are all in bloom. How ironic, this being the day of your dad's funeral. It is truly a sign."

Since that day, I've come to learn that when a loved one dies, we experience unmeasurable grief, and we are pulled out of our comfort zone for a purpose. As time goes on and God begins to heal our broken hearts, we can remember all the wonderful times and be filled with joy. Time does heals all wounds.

Know that if you are experiencing grief today, things will get better. Even though you will always miss your loved one, this grief is but for a season. You will again experience joy, and my prayer is that the joy of the Lord will live on in your heart, always.

Chapter 17
The Owl and Its Miracles

One of the most important feelings to have is a satisfaction with life. Those who appreciate the value their life has to themselves and to others, enjoy life more. Recognizing that your life has meaning and that you make a difference can help lessen your anxiety about death.

— Lon G. Nungesser

You would know the secret of death.

But how shall you find it unless you seek it in the heart of life?

The owl whose night-bound eyes are blind unto the day cannot unveil the mystery of light.

If you would indeed behold the spirit of death, open your heart wide unto the body of life,

For life and earth are one, even as the river and sea are one.

— Khalil Gibran

My father's favourite celebration in the entire year was Christmas. And one of my father's most loved hobbies was woodworking. I find this resemblance both comforting and surprisingly remarkable, knowing Jesus, who was born on Christmas, was also a carpenter.

There wasn't anything Dad couldn't fix, or build. One Christmas, just like the traditional Santa Claus, he made all the things a little girl needed for her dolls: a cradle, high-chair, table and chairs. He must have worked down in his workshop like Santa every night after I was safely tucked into bed. Dad also *mastered* the art of woodcarving. It was incredible the things he could carve out of a solid block of wood. He made ducks and loons, nutcrackers, Indians and owls. He always particularly liked owls, and he once gave me one with marbles for the eyes.

Five months after my father's death, we took a trip to Europe that ended in Scotland, which was fittingly the country of his heritage. I was amazed because everywhere we travelled, I saw owls. This was another sign, I believe, that was prompted by my angels, who wanted to show me my dad was still with me, in that first year, guiding me along my way. (Since then I've heard people tell me their signs have been butterflies and specific birds like robins and hummingbirds).

As we came home to celebrate Christmas that year, the owls kept showing me their magic, and I must tell you this story: we decorated the house, set up the Christmas tree and wrapped the gifts. It wasn't easy, as I had little enthusiasm about this celebration at this time of year. Anniversaries of any kind are forever difficult, but the ones which occur in the very first year after a death are painfully fresh.

Imagining the holidays ahead and how this year was going to be different preyed on my heart as I reminisced about happier times. It's difficult to imagine the holidays without our loved ones, and it's difficult to accept that life doesn't ever stay the same and that your life will never be the same without your loved one.

I knew we all had no choice but to find our new normal; we knew there was still life for all of us to be lived. I know Dad would tell us to grasp God's hand for dear life and trust Him to guide us into the ever-evolving future. But I was moments away from the angels guiding me.

Days before, I had shared the overseas owl stories with a dear childhood friend over the telephone. A few days later, the doorbell rang, and she appeared delivering an owl Christmas tree ornament. It was a pretty, white, sparkly glass globe with an owl in the centre.

One evening, I realized that life was moving forward, even if I was stuck. I knew Christmas coming was not an option. And then something really bizarre happened while we were decorating the tree.

I began by digging out all the new decorations first. As I selected each ornament, I looked at the pictures on top of the fireplace and reflected on the lives of my loved ones as I said a silent prayer, putting each ornament on the tree in front of me.

John and I then stopped and got ready to attend the 5:00 p.m. Mass at our local parish. When we came back, we turned on some soft Christmas background music, placed some pizza in the oven, poured something to drink and resumed putting the rest of the ornaments on the Christmas tree. I was feeling really sad and didn't want to even think about Christmas decorations. "I'm not into this," I thought. "I don't want to be doing this. I'm too sad." Nike had left us December 16th the year before and with Christmas being my dad's favourite holiday it all seemed empty. The darkness of the shorter days also set the mood.

Then, all of a sudden, in the middle of despair, I could hear my dad's voice say to me, "You can't do this, Kate. You can't be like that. You have to be there for your children and grandchildren. You have to go on and live your life. That's how it works."

This was something he would remind us about quite often. And at that precise moment, you will never guess what happened! At that very moment, the owl ornament dropped from the Christmas tree! It was the same thing that happened the previous year, when Nike's ornament fell off the tree! Luckily, this ornament did not break. That's when I knew God had sent His angels to us, and it would not surprise me if they were also guided by my dad.

After all the decorations were hung on the tree, John put all the boxes away and found a program to watch on television. I decided to telephone my friend to share this remarkable event. I also talked to her about Advent and how a difficult family situation manifested this last week and how it seemed to test my faith. I always believed family was the oldest unit in humanity, the bedrock of our society. Many of us have dysfunction in our families, but the way it is supposed to work is like this: when everyone else has abandoned you, you can count on your family. In faith, it's easy because our spiritual family is our father, God; our brother, Jesus; the Holy Spirit; and our mother, Mary, who is always there for us!

Sometimes, having faith, though, isn't all black and white; but when it isn't clear, I resort to prayer to get the answers. Those who complain the most, accomplish the least. Love the people in your life who treat you right, and pray for the ones who don't. Don't let the shadows of the past darken the doorstep of your future. This family circumstance took a lot of energy, and I was hurt badly, but prayer told me that forgiveness was a much better option because a grudge is the heaviest thing you will ever carry.

We should always remember forgiveness is not an emotion. Like love, it is an act of the will. We can't choose how we feel, but we can choose how we act! Forgiveness is not always easy, and sometimes it feels more painful than the wound we suffered from the one who inflicted it. Yet there is no peace without forgiveness. Forgiveness, in God's view, restores life. When you forgive, you don't change the past; you change the future—so don't deny yourself the best future! You get a second chance every second!

As hard as we all try, it seems inevitable that we will reach a time when we turn our backs on Him. That's where mercy and forgiveness come in. No matter how bad we are, no matter how egregious the sin, God is always ready and willing to welcome us back. He also gives us the grace to share His mercy with others. All we have to do is have a repentant spirit to help us to acknowledge our sins and give us a firm purpose of amendment.

Perhaps the devil's pronounced curse is to make us believe we have nothing for which to repent, but we know God's love is unconditional. God loves us no matter what. However, our salvation is conditional. And the first condition is repentance. When Jesus began His public ministry, His first word was "repent." He repeated this message, over and over. If we fail to repent, God will still love us. But we won't be spending eternity with Him.

That same evening, after an hour of telephone conversation and a few tears and few laughs with a dear friend, we said our good nights. I then pulled out my laptop to answer a few e-mails before I decided to retire to bed myself. It was then I thought the angels also had gone to bed.

While sitting quietly in the room by myself, as the Christmas tree lights were sparkling, I started to type. All of a sudden, I heard a soft *ping!* Immediately I stared up at the tree, and in a soft whisper I said to myself, "What was that?" I set my laptop on the coffee table in front of me and walked toward the Christmas tree. Slowly, my eyes gazed at the spot where the owl and the cat decorations hung. My eyes were surveying the tree branches as though they were under a microscope, searching for the answer for this mysterious, gentle sound. I noticed an ornament had fallen just above the owl and the new angel cat ornament. It was a pewter snowflake ornament. But guess what the inscription on it said! "Faith brings miracles."

Quite a magical night!

Just remember to keep the faith. Anything is possible, as I believe we are all surrounded by angels, even guardian angels, who see us all as equals: rich or poor, great or small, in sickness or in health, talented or handicapped, leaders or followers, saints or sinners. To them, we are all precious souls, and their love never fails us. It's not impossible for God, in His wisdom, to send angels to intervene in the affairs of men. Perhaps you have had an angelic encounter in your life with one of these Heavenly messengers. Never minimize their powers. If you haven't had such an encounter, don't be surprised if some day you do, for you must remember nothing is impossible for God.

Chapter 18
Touched by an Angel

God didn't promise days without pain, laughter without sorrow or sun without rain. But He did promise strength for the day, comfort for the tears and light for the way. If God brings you to it, He will bring you through it.

— Unknown

Only a few months into my cancer journey, I received a phone call from Karen, a friend who had recently been diagnosed with breast cancer. She was calling me to help prepare herself for the emotional experience of losing her hair along with her dignity. This story, I believe, offers a spiritual perspective that transforms even the darkest situations.

The one difference I had heard between she and I was that she was very angry and mad at God for what she was now going through. She was the textbook candidate they tell you about—the one who experiences all the steps that lead up to acceptance—and for her, God wasn't on her side. In her mind, God was responsible, and He was who she blamed. She was five years younger than I. It also didn't help that her husband had decided to leave her during this journey, making the uphill climb 100 times more difficult for her. She was alone, without a loving partner supporting her and being by her side. I truly can't imagine her marathon.

Our paths occasionally crossed, and eventually we both came out the other side as two changed souls. I was now heartbroken to hear that, once again, this beautiful woman was told she'd have to do battle one more time.

During this second battle, I was delighted to hear she was not angry at God in the same way anymore and that she had found peace through God. The Bible teaches, very clearly, that there are indeed spirit beings who can connect with and appear in our physical world. The Bible identifies these beings as angels. Angels are spirit beings who are faithful in serving God. Angels are righteous, good and holy.

On a trip south to an island with a friend, before her chemotherapy was about to begin once again, Karen felt God's holy hands upon her shoulders right above the place her cancer had returned. Later, she asked her friend, who had accompanied her there to the island, if she had placed her hands upon her that afternoon while resting by the ocean. Karen discovered this was not the case. She said it was something she could hardly explain, but she remembered a feeling of total peace coming over her entire being. The horrific fear of the cancer returning had left her.

Now, I know you are thinking this story is all hearsay and unsupported by real physical evidence. In our world, it's always easier to put these feelings or experiences off to imagination, but I dare you to argue with anyone who has truly experienced a Divine intervention and is convinced of it.

Of course, it is only human to want to see proof before believing. But it's so unfortunate people have gotten so wrapped up in religious superstition and dogma that it makes them resistant to believing anything without hard scientific evidence. In our everyday lives, we do not need proof to believe in something. In fact, in our natural world, if the weatherman says there is a 60 percent chance of rain, do you need proof before you are justified in bringing an umbrella with you?

Hours later, these two women went up to their room and dressed for dinner. As they were coming down to the lobby, they decided to stop and take a couple of photographs of each other. Better still, there was a third acquaintance they had met, and she was willing to take the photograph of the two ladies together.

This room was simple, and the light was balanced throughout. All three friends confirmed that what they then saw had nothing to do with the room, the light, the camera card or the picture itself. And the photo had not been enhanced in any way. Even the woman taking the picture said she didn't see anything unusual at the time she was looking through the viewfinder. But later, when the photograph was examined, they could see gold bright angel wings above Karen's shoulders! (The colour copy of this photograph is breathtaking compared to the black-and-white on page 264.)

It was truly astounding. And it was all the proof I needed. The memory of the halo that I experienced after my car accident came rushing back to me.

Karen told me this story in her own precise words. She made sure I had this photograph and has given me permission to write this chapter and print this photograph of her blessed encounter with Christ. To this day, we have both participated in the CIBC Run for the Cure, and she has been involved in many marathons. She truly is my hero and exemplifies pure bravery. She has endured so much, yet has shown such courage and strength, both physically and spiritually.

Sadly, her cancer has returned, and I am told the prognosis is not good.

All her friends and colleagues share in our prayers and pledge in our faith that she will continue to be touched by God's hands and the angel wings that protect her. Thank you, my friend, for allowing me to share your most precious and private story. Please know I will never stop praying for you!

Chapter 19
The Last Awakening

Along the Road

I walked a mile with Pleasure;
She chatted all the way;
But left me none the wiser
For all she had to say.

I walked a mile with Sorrow,
And ne'er a word said she;
But, oh! The things I learned from her,
When sorrow walked with me.

— Robert Browning Hamilton

It was a beautiful sunny day, too beautiful to waste sitting at a desk, so I escaped out of the concrete building into the fresh smell of autumn. The leaves were turning crimson, and the sun felt warm on my face.

As I was walking back from posting a letter to my son, my thoughts focused on dedicating prayers to a co-worker's ill friend and for the health of my own aunt. I felt myself turning into the grounds of St. Peter's Cathedral built in the 13th-century French Gothic style. Built in 1885, it was the third church to occupy the site; the original dating from 1834.

I looked up at the two Gothic gargoyles alongside the façade and pulled the heavy wooden double door toward me. As I opened it, I saw a long aisle which led to God's altar. I had been in this church many times, and as I walked in, I touched the holy water and made the sign of the cross. Nearing the altar, I noticed a few scattered souls praying among the pews throughout the holy space. I ignored but respected their presence as I quietly selected my own place of silence. As I sat down and pulled down the kneeler, the bench creaked, and the sounds echoed throughout the church.

I kneeled down and started praying, thanking God for my blessings. Then I began to pray for those who were facing challenges. But in this moment, tears rolled down my cheeks, and I began to ask our Lord God to help grant me the desire of my heart. This request even surprised me, as it had been quite some time since I had placed myself before others in my prayers, but I have always understood that as we grow in faith and love, we'll find that the desire of our hearts matches up with the desire of God's heart.

I had been having some serious health issues the previous three months, so I believe that my own needs came to the forefront. After my discussion with God, I quietly left the cathedral and returned to the sunshine outside the walls of God's dwelling.

I walked by the location in the park, adjacent to the church, where I had passed out three months earlier during my lunchtime. I had just finished enjoying a shiny red apple for lunch while reading a chapter in a book that my father and I had talked about four days before his fatal heart attack.

It was called *The Boy Who Met Jesus,* by Immaculée Ilibagiza. As noted on the back cover, it's a story of a shepherd boy named Segatashya who was "born into a penniless and illiterate pagan family in the most remote region of Rwanda. He never attended school, never saw a Bible and never set foot in a church. Then one summer day, in 1982, while Segatashya was resting beneath a shade tree, Jesus Christ paid him a visit. Jesus asked the startled teenager if he'd undertake a mission to remind mankind how to reach Heaven. Segatashya accepted the assignment on the condition Jesus answered all his questions about faith, religion, the purpose of life, and the nature of Heaven and hell. Jesus agreed, and the young man set off on one of the most miraculous journeys in modern history."

I finished reading my chapter and stared at the mature oak tree in front of the picnic table where I had been sitting reading my book. I began to whisper as my eyes focused on the tree, imagining how Segatashya must have felt when Christ appeared to him. "Oh, Lord, I wish you could someday appear to me like that!" I said. "How staggering that would be to be able to see you and sit and have a conversation outside of prayer, just like you did with your followers nearly 2,000 years ago."

I continued, "You know I am writing my book for exactly the same reason. People need to discern your voice over the noise of our busy daily lives. I so wish you could give me another sign."

With that, I closed my book and stood up. I turned around to look for a trash container where I could to leave my apple core. The nearest one was quite a distance away, in the opposite direction, so I decided to take it with me instead.

As I took about six steps toward the road to cross over to work, my vision suddenly blurred, and it felt like someone was pulling me down from my shoulders onto the grass. I had fainted before, but this time felt very different and came on me abruptly, without warning.

As I lay on the grass, I realized that no one seemed to notice! I thought, "What is wrong with this world that no one notices anyone in distress?" But I also wondered, was God answering my request to "give me another sign?" I know it is always easier to put these things off to other causes like dehydration or heat stroke. But I had been reading in the shade. A kind woman walked me back to work. The doctor said there was no medical explanation for what had happened to me.

Three months earlier, I started having vertigo and other health issues. The most recent episode involved an alarming rise in my blood pressure and heart/pulse rate. My arms went numb, my head was pounding, and I could hear my heart beat through my ears. It was like someone had knocked the wind out of me, and I could barely take a breath. It was all I could do to unlock the front door of our home, and I called an ambulance for myself because I felt this could be the early signs of a stroke.

After a battery of tests—blood work, enzyme checks, EKGs, chest X-rays, 24-hour monitors, an echogram and a trail of cardiac tests—they changed my beta-blocker medication but found no apparent reason for these conditions, other than diagnosing me with post-traumatic stress disorder accompanied by sinus tachycardia, which mimicked arrhythmia. The rhythm of my normal resting heart rate had elevated out of control. This happened because my body had reached its maximum threshold for anxiety and grief. (Feelings that are born out of negative thinking for too long create accumulative anxiety.)

Since then, I've learned anxiety is not a weakness; it can be caused by trying to cope with life's many pressures and deep grief. My polished identity had now spun out of control and changed its status to "vulnerable."

Then came what I like to call "The Last Awakening." It came as a telephone call on November 13, 2014, exactly five years to the day on the same telephone on which I had been told I had breast cancer. I can still hear the message: "Mrs. Hyland, this is the doctor who released you from the hospital emergency this morning. We don't want to alarm you, but the radiologist who read your chest X-ray noted what appeared to be a concern given your past history, which warrants a repeat X-ray."

After going for another X-ray, the second radiologist confirmed what appeared to be a nodal on the opposite side of my chest, this time not in the breast but in the chest itself, between the first and second rib bone. As I hung up the receiver, I literally fell to my knees shaking. I was certain I could surely overcome a heart scare with the right medication, by incorporating an exercise regimen into my lifestyle, changing my diet and reducing the anxiety in my life. What I wasn't certain about was whether my heart— and mind—could win another victory over cancer.

The words from the doctors five years ago rang in my head: "If it is to return, it will be sooner rather than later, and it will be someplace different."

In between deep breaths, I reminded myself of my third vision, when Christ fought with the demons and pulled the cancer from me. I kept telling myself, "Kate, have faith. You know what you saw and felt, and you know it was Jesus who gave you a second chance to make good on your life, and you have."

We are all human, and humans slide into fear quite easily, especially when it comes to life-threatening situations. My faith told me that I was going to be all right and that Jesus was with me, but my fear told me that I may not see my children marry and have children of their own and that my husband and I may never fulfill our dreams of retirement together. I kept trying to focus on my vision and uphold my strong faith in the Holy Spirit. I was remembering the words "The Lord is near to all who call upon Him, to all who call upon Him in truth" (Psalm 145:18).

That night, when I turned out the lights, the clock displayed 11:56 p.m. In the morning, when I awoke, the clock displayed 6:52 a.m. I thought, "The **13**s are back after about a year. My angels are back watching over me yet again."

By 3:00 in the afternoon, my doctor called, and as he spoke, his words were the most glorious words I swear I have ever heard: "Good news—there doesn't appear to be a reoccurrence of the cancer. It looks to be okay."

My husband and I cried with this news, although at the same time I'm ashamed to admit I was upset with myself for not trusting what God had already shown me. Be careful of those demons carrying fear!

As I hung up the telephone, I was reminded of a story called "God Granting Miracles." It was about a religious man on top of a roof during a great flood. A man comes by in a boat and says, "Get in, get in!" The religious man replies, "No, I'll be fine. I have faith in God. He will grant me a miracle."

Later, the water rises up to his waist, and another boat comes by, and another man tells him to get in the boat. He responds, again, that he has great faith in God, and he is convinced God will give him a miracle. With the water at about chest height, another boat comes to rescue him, but again, he turns down the offer because he believes God will grant him a miracle and save him.

With the water at chin height, a helicopter throws down a ladder, and they tell him one last time, "Get in!" Mumbling, with the water in his mouth, he again turns down the request for help because of his faith in God. With this, he drowns.

When he arrives at the gates of Heaven, with broken faith, he says to Peter, "I really thought God would grant me a miracle, and I have been let down." St. Peter chuckles and responds, "I don't know what you're complaining about. He sent you three boats and a helicopter."

Sometimes, our prayers are not answered the way we expect them to be, but they are answered the way God chooses. We also don't always have the good sense to recognize God is answering our prayers, but it is up to us to move our feet and trust in Him. I believe this was one of those times in my life. I am convinced this is another fine example of God working in mysterious ways, answering our prayers in different ways from what we expect.

In another story, "Interview with God", a man asks God "What surprises you most about mankind? God's reply is this: "Many things. That they get bored of being children, are in a rush to grow up, and then long to be children again. That they lose their health to make money and then lose their money to restore health. That by thinking anxiously about the future, they forget the present, and live neither for the present nor for the future. That they live as if they will never die, and die as if they had never lived."

What does this say? We must live one day at a time, in the *present moment.*

For me, God was telling me that I had to make some monumental changes if I wanted to live healthier and longer without heart problems or the cancer returning. If you don't take the rest you need, your body will eventually force you to take it by getting sick.

Perhaps He has been giving me signs to start silencing the mind and allowing the soul to heal itself. Perhaps He did hear my meek cry to have pity on me when I was in prayer in the basilica that fine day, or He was listening to me beside that oak tree in the park. Perhaps He has sent me some boats! We can't avoid pressure in life, but we should always remember that whatever crisis we face is God's way of reshaping our stubborn, self-willed hearts into models of perseverance and character. Perhaps it was time to release stress, heal and trust.

In times when we feel beaten down by our weakness, when we "hit rock bottom," as it were, physically or mentally, it is only then can we realize we need some help. And sometimes, our health forces us to take a road our brains would have told us to not take. It is then we need an injection of strength. That injection of strength is called *grace*. And when we accept God's grace, we need nothing more. After all, His grace is sufficient.

Somehow my first vision always brings me back to reality and gives me clarity: "Let go and let God." We need to remind ourselves to live for today, because that is the only day we can be really sure of.

Chapter 20
Calm My Fears, Increase My Trust

Know Christ, know peace. No Christ, no peace.

— Unknown

When I started this book, I didn't see this chapter coming. I never knew I would be fortunate enough to have another vision, let alone while I was writing this book. It happened in the early hours of January 31, 2015. Being openly receptive and consciously aware, I believe I was blessed once again to see God's love.

The previous evening, I made a long-distance telephone call to my mother's youngest sister, who had been suddenly widowed. It had been a month since I had last spoken to her, and I wanted to know how she was managing since I last saw her, at her husband's funeral. We talked for over an hour, and she left me with a simple two-line prayer given to her by Elaine, her devoted and closest girlfriend, whom she had known for over 60 years, a woman I also knew.

It had been easy to find Elaine at the funeral. All I'd had to do was search the room for the angel, and her sincere and natural glow of caring and love would radiate through her physical presence. She was one of the most beautiful souls I have ever known. As she greeted me, she reminded me she still had a prayer group praying for me. I was taken aback by her comment, as it had been five years since the first onset of my cancer, but it really didn't surprise me, knowing her soul and the fact that she, too, had recently lost a daughter to breast cancer. Elaine isn't one to pray "once and done" like too many of us do.

As I talked to my dear aunt, she told me about the prayer Elaine had shared with her, which was simple and sweet and something anyone can say at any place or any time. She said, "It isn't complicated or hard to remember." My aunt told me this prayer had helped her through some difficult hours while she watched her husband struggle for his last breath, as it took him three weeks to die of lung cancer. She also said that during those three weeks, she passed this simple prayer along to several people at the hospital she had met who were either dealing with cancer themselves or who were there with a loved one. I wrote it down.

I turned in to bed that evening and lay there thinking about the magnificent gift my aunt had given to me moments before, not imagining the meaning of her short prayer would be the meaning of my next vision from God. For weeks, I had been praying to God, asking Him to present another vision to me. I told Him, in prayer, that I was ready, as it had been a while, and I reassured Him He knew the vision would be safe with me.

I never felt doubtful, and I always understood what the visions meant, so I explained how blessed I would feel to be given another message from Him and how I was ready this time.

After I saw my Lord, my eyes opened wide. My first vision had been in 1990. I looked over at the clock on my night table. The numbers showed 3:46 a.m. My first thought was "Of course the angels are surrounding me again."

The moment I opened my eyes, my husband reached over and touched me. He said he felt the precise moment I had awakened, as the sound of my breathing had changed. The only words I could mutter to him, in a soft, low voice, were "I had another vision." This time, he responded with silence, letting me take it all in.

The vision was as pure and simple as the reflection of the two-line prayer: "Calm my fears. Increase my trust."

I was in what felt like a car or a vehicle. I don't remember the car moving or me driving it, but I remember the front windshield and that I was holding onto the steering wheel. (I interpret being in a car as being in a place where you move forward.) This time, what was most important was the rear-view mirror to my right.

When I had seen my dad in a vision three months after his passing, I had also been in what felt like a car, only I'd seen no car interior, steering wheel or mirrors. Dad had just been moving at the same pace beside me. (I often wonder if cars played a part in my connection with Dad because he was the one who taught me how to drive. Perhaps it became our private place, sealed away from the distraction of others.)

The only similarity between these two visions was that no words needed to be spoken. In His presence, your soul is in complete peace and is joyous.

This time, staring into the rear-view mirror, I clearly saw the face of Jesus Christ looking back at me! I was startled, and I felt like I was jumping backward in fear or shock. I wasn't afraid of Jesus himself, but I remember feeling fear and being afraid, as this image appeared so suddenly in a place I was so totally not expecting. But as I stared back at His face, I knew immediately I was in His presence, because a complete and all-embracing relief poured over my soul.

There was nothing fearful there. Jesus's beard and long, dark hair flowed past the mirror's limited view, but the details of His face were breathtaking and magical. The complexion of His face was soft, warm and perfectly flawless, and His face was vibrantly alive. It was like His skin glowed; there was a soft sunshine emanating from within His body, which was bronze in colour yet a tone unknown on Earth.

His eyes were as clear and blue as the most beautiful blue sky or ocean I had ever set my eyes on anywhere in the world. His eyes were very gentle, firm and steadfast, radiating a soft source of pure light for which I did not even have to squint. It was an all-consuming, forgiving love, one that overwhelmed me, and I felt like it drowned every cell of my being with reassuring love and peace. It left me with no uncertainty, which was a feeling I recognized from before.

In fact, the light seemed to absorb back into my eyes with the most calming quality I had ever known. The transformation of one's heart and one's being is hard to describe in human words, no matter what language we use.

Then Jesus shook His head slowly, from left to right, while His eyes remained soothingly fixed on my eyes. It felt like He was smiling at me, but it was His love smiling through His eyes.

Immediately, I felt my fear lift away from me, and that same sense of peace came over me. It was as if it was swallowing me up, inside out. I remembered this feeling from the first vision, as it had been something too powerful and God-given to ever forget even after **23** years.

As soon as I absorbed this "calmness" of peace, Jesus nodded His head up and down, indicating "yes." He was reassuring me that by surrendering my fears to Him, I had earned the ultimate peace from Him. He was telling me to know that His love was real and eternal and that it was mine to have if I loved Him and did His Will on Earth.

Ask Him into your heart, and He will refuse you nothing, for the one truth you should know and celebrate in your life is "Jesus loves you."

It was then I felt a human compulsion to glance over to the front windshield so I could see where I was driving. I was also thinking that I shouldn't dare take my eyes off Jesus, but I still thought I should see where I was going.

I looked back to the rear-view mirror, and sadly, Jesus's image had disappeared. This was the moment my eyes opened, and I found myself once again staring at the ceiling above my bed, lying there in a motionless state. My heart felt a pang of disappointment for having changed my focus, and all I could do was replay what I had just seen over and over again in my mind. As I did it, the two-line prayer was clearly in front of me.

"Calm my fears. Increase my trust."

For fear was what I'd first felt when I saw Jesus, and as He felt my sudden fear, He nodded. "No. Do not be afraid."

As I focused on His eyes and face, I recognized Him, and I *knew* it was Jesus. The familiar, incredible peace and calmness came over me like a deep, all-consuming wave.

As Jesus is all-knowing, I knew then He felt my calmness and He recognized my "increased trust" in Him. That is when He nodded "yes" and again smiled at me.

He had increased my trust in Him on a more profound and unfathomable level. After all, this was the second time He had revealed himself to me in a vision. I knew it was our one Lord and Saviour—no doubts, no question and with absolute certainty.

In fact, He had answered my prayer. He had trusted what I had asked Him, which was to give me another act of faith to "increase my trust." Only this time, I knew what to do with it, unlike **23** years ago. I was to share it in my book for you and for the world.

Forever thanks with my sincere love to my Aunt Clare and Elaine for leading me to become refreshed and renewed.

Chapter 21
The Message—Plant the
Seed—Why Me?

Again He said, "What shall we say the kingdom of God is like, or what parable shall we use to describe it? It is like a mustard seed, which is the smallest seed you plant in the ground. Yet when planted, it grows and becomes the largest of all garden plants, with such big branches that the birds of the air can perch in its shade."

—Mark 4:30

One fine morning, when I climbed into the car, one of the first messages I felt was "Ask and you shall receive. Whatever you ask in my name, this I will do, that the Father may be glorified in the Son. If you ask me anything in my name, I will do it" (John 14:**13**–14).

I understood Jesus spoke time and again about the need for faith. So whatever we ask, I knew we must ask in faith. Secondly, if we grow in faith and trust (which I felt I had), our prayers will change from asking what we want to asking in the name of Jesus ("If it be your Will, Father . . ."). When we ask for what God wants instead of what we want, then our prayers will be answered.

Immediately, I started talking to God, saying, "Well, Lord, I have my chapters, I have my cover, I have my title. And if this is truly the message you've been showing me all along, for **23** years, because you want me to share it, I need to ask you to help me find my author. I know it will likely be the hardest part, so yes, I need your help . . . if it is your Will."

Then I got desperate and started talking to God like a friend: "I'm hitting a wall right now, so please talk to me. I'm listening. I promised you I would do your work, but you need to give me the tools to help me deliver it, and right now, I need the right author, editor and publisher who can deliver the message the way it was intended to be delivered through me from you."

So one week after my father's death, I tried to contact a well-known author of similar material. During that process, it turned out I received an e-mail from Erica McKenzie— someone else who had seen my post and who was apparently in the process of writing her own book, claiming she had died 11 years ago and had visited Heaven (her book, *Dying to Fit In,* was published in May 2015). It was in that moment, I knew Erica had been placed in my path for a reason. My heart was telling me I was on a special mission and I felt protective in carrying these delicate messages. I told her I knew nothing about writing, editing and publishers, and her advice was, "Well, yes, you will have a lot to learn, but I can help you with all that."

In one of our conversations, she kindly said, "To answer your question of how I found my author and my team, I want you to listen to what I am going to tell you, because it is important. I can feel, without knowing your story, how deep your passion runs, and I also happen to know you speak the truth. You know your story is a gift for you from

God, so when I tell you God literally brought my people to me that are my team to help me with my story, I want you to have peace that this is also how it must happen for you.

I am going to caution you, as you proceed, to keep praying as you have been and to remember we must find a way to let go and let God bring things all together in His timing."

She continued, saying, "Sometimes, as humans, this is really hard to do, but we must be patient, because when we use the faith to sustain us, He will never let us down. I witnessed a lot, like the countless people before me who have been so brave to come forward to tell their stories, but before I arrived to where I am now, I had to work so hard for so many years and be faced with much rejection. It's hard when you just want to tell your story and use your gift God has given you, but it is possible."

She continued with her advice. "Now that I am finally where I am today, I vowed I will never forget how hard I had to work, and I want to help the people coming after me, in hopes I can help make their journey easier. I suggest you pray about speaking with me, and after, be quiet and listen to what God has to say."

Then she said the most thought-provoking words: "You may find this hard to believe, but you are likely the best person to write your own story. You will just need help in getting it out from you to the world." She concluded by saying she hoped her advice was helpful, and she said, "I am here if you would like for me to try to help."

A few weeks later, we finally had an in-depth conversation over the telephone. After our conversation, these were her words, in a follow-up e-mail:

> *I want to tell you how wonderful it was to speak with you today as your words speak the truth. You are doing such a wonderful job, Kate, being quiet, and listening to Him that having the patience will become easier as*

you continue to write down everything. The death of your father is an entirely new testimony. You will be able to be there for so many that have had, and are going through, loss. This is an important part of your journey. It's really quite beautiful how He has chosen to use you on so many levels to reach the multitudes. Up to now, I feel your book hasn't happened yet because your father's death is going to be a big part of your book.

Remember, you have the gift of message through your visions, numbers, cancer, your cat and your dad's passing. Do you see how all this is unfolding? Your book needs to include in it what you're going through now, as a result of his passing. What you are seeing now, and what you are feeling now. How your relationship is developing with your Dad in his new role as he has crossed over. You are stronger than you give your human self-credit for.

God wants to give you another gift, Kate, but you must do the work first. YOU CAN DO ALL THINGS THROUGH CHRIST WHO STRENGTHENS YOU!!

I feel if you continued to let me help you, and keep writing about what you are going through, like I said, you will be ready to put it into the right hands this year. Hold close to your heart, as I told you, He wants to surround you with the group of people that will not only help you tell your story, and allow you to keep it in your words, but it is also important in the fact these people will provide support, and help you grow, and develop your gifts.

When we come together, with all our different gifts, we will accomplish great things for HIM. I promise you, if you would like, I will hold your hand, and help ensure this happens for you. Keep praying, and remember,

God hears you and does bring into our lives the help to
be the tangible bridge between Heaven and Earth so we
may in turn serve in our calling.

After receiving this advice, I spent many hours talking and praying to God, feeling humbled for the gift that I could be the vessel to deliver His message. I believe many are called, but few will listen. Sometimes when things like rejection happen, we as humans think of it as if we did something wrong, or maybe we failed in some way, or we weren't good enough. But the real answer is that rejection is God's way of protecting us. If we listen, He uses it to lead us in the right direction—a direction that is part of His plan. God has been calling me for a very long time.

On a beautiful autumn day, October **13**, 2012, John and I drove to a town called St. Jacob's. It is the centre of the Amish Mennonite community in Ontario. We always love to visit its huge outdoor market, which includes unique shops and stands indoors and a small outlet mall. Back in town, there is my favourite Angel store and a place that sells homemade kitchen trinkets and preserves.

At lunch time, we drove to Anna Mae's Bakery and Restaurant in Millbank, Ontario, another familiar stop on many of our trips in this vicinity. We have taken close friends and my parents there often for lunch. We love the home style meals with roasted chicken, real mashed potatoes, buttery carrots and cheese bread. They also sell jams, crafts, books and bakery items.

While we were waiting to be seated, we sat in the room which was lined with handmade wooden benches. We were still reeling from the news we had received earlier that day. While I was taking photographs in a quaint church yard, John received a phone call. A tragic car accident had taken the life of a beloved friend and co-worker the previous evening. With dear Maureen on my mind, my eyes focused across the aisle to some spiritual books displayed in freestanding wired stands right in front of me. I walked over, and for the first time, I felt like I set my eyes on my destiny.

I leafed through these countless books written by authors who had come before me, people who have been so brave to come forward to tell their stories just as my new friend had told me.

Within two weeks, I was carrying one of these books onto a jumbo jet bound for Israel, on our Holy Land Pilgrimage from November 1st through 13th.

From that time, I continued to ask God to direct me. I had the chapters, the cover, the title and a lot of the material already written by then. I realized I needed an editor, perhaps more than even a writer. I never stopped praying for God's direction. I remembered being told by my new author friend that, two days after she was about to give up on her book, her author and her team appeared, so I stayed focused and hopeful every day.

By now, praying seemed to be taking over my every thought. The next day, while walking into work after praying through the park, I ran into another friend from work, and we talked briefly about my father's passing. As we talked and hugged, she commented, "I think you can write this yourself. After all, the Bible stories were written by ordinary people, and you are an angel, my friend." That was not the first time someone had called me that! She said, "I think you have been carefully chosen because you are a simple seeking soul who has a pure heart, with pure motives in seeking the truth of God."

A month later, upon my return from Israel, I entered my favourite local Christian book and gift store. I decided to ask the friendly woman behind the counter if they had a list of local Christian authors. She gave me some names, and one of these authors returned my call and granted me the most engaging and encouraging interview, in the most personal place possible—her very own home—on May **23**, 2013.

When I met the author, Mary, I told her that I needed to find that perfect author, the person I've been praying for each day, to deliver my message the way God intended me to. Mary's advice was simple and reinforced what others were telling me. She said, "You are the best person to write your story. Your passion comes from within. Believe in yourself, and write this book yourself."

Earlier that same week, before the interview, something happened that was equally as inspiring. My mother gave me a pendant of the Virgin Mary, one that had been on one of my Grandmother Rose's necklaces from Italy. I placed this pendant on my gold chain around my neck. After the interview, I couldn't help but wonder about the significance of the name Mary. I wondered, "Has Mother Mary also been mysteriously guiding me along my way here?"

The word *believe* was also written on Dad's baseball hat, the one I had given him when I had my cancer. It was from the 2010 Winter Olympics. I also have several Christmas ornaments which are inscribed with the word *believe*. It was important advice, but it had taken me a long time to take it.

I was also reminded of my father's letters, which I'd found **13** days into our grief. Dad had written down his personal thoughts, memories, advice and poetry, and he left me with these encouraging and inspiring words: "Nothing beats you. You finish what you start."

When I left my parents' apartment after reading my father's intimate thoughts, it finally occurred to me: Dad wrote all the time. What a gift! I have followed in his footsteps and have written down my thoughts about faith, all the messages I have received, and the visions that I saw.

The rest is history. I gave up on finding an author. These words are mine with the help of God. Once I stopped searching for a publisher, several publishers appeared who shared the same vision, mission and values. A voice told me I had to trust the one that seemed to be the right fit and with that right fit, came that perfect editor who was passionately gifted to help me tell my compelling story of God's grace.

On a trip to Turkey, I met a precious woman who almost became a nun. She gave me the same advice as my author friend: "Remember, you must find a way to let go and let God bring things altogether in His timing."

They were all right. God *was* waiting for me to write it. God has put me on this path for **23** years. I was meant to share my story with you so that you, too, can be open to these mysteries. My story is not meant to be debated, nor is it meant to present adversarial arguments. Besides I'm not a confrontational person. I've just wrote the stories the way they happened to me.

These days, I don't think much about the devil, his wickedness and evil spirit. I'm sure he would try to convince me it would be easier to give up on this mission. So with devoted perseverance and endurance—and God's love and strength surrounding me—I give you my most personal experiences.

Father, help us not to be quitters. Give us the strength to endure to the end, where eternal life with you awaits us. Amen.

Chapter 22
A Good Man

Then Jesus declared, "I am the bread of life. He who comes to me will never go hungry, and He who believes in me, will never be thirsty. But as I told you, you have seen me and still you do not believe. All that the Father gives me will come to me, and whoever comes to me I will never drive away. For I have come down from Heaven not to do my will but to do the will of Him who sent me. And this is the will of Him who sent me, that I shall lose none of all that He has given me, but raise them up at the last day. For my Father's Will is that everyone who looks to the Son and believes in Him shall have eternal life, and I will raise him up at the last day."

—John 6:35

The good man walks along in the ever-brightening light of God's favor; the dawn gives way to morning splendor.

—Proverbs 4:18

Everyone described my dad as "a good man." We heard this time and time again during his life and also many times after his passing. In our eyes, he truly was a saint.

One Friday evening, in the dark on September 28, 2012, I found an American penny on a sidewalk. It had two crosses imprinted, one on each side. I viewed this as a unique gift that continually shares a meaningful message. It's a reminder of Jesus Christ and all that He's done for me. It reminded me of a poem I once read which parallels the symbolism of my **13**s. It's by Verna Mae Thomas, and it is called "The Cross in My Pocket." It goes like this:

I carry a cross in my pocket,
A simple reminder to me
Of the fact I am a Christian,
No matter where I may be.

This little cross is not magic,
Nor is it a good luck charm.
It isn't meant to protect me
From every physical harm.

It's not for identification
For all the world to see.
It's simply an understanding
Between my Savior and me.

When I put my hand in my pocket
To bring out a coin or a key,
The cross is there to remind me
Of the price He paid for me.

It reminds me, too, to be thankful
For my blessings day by day
And to strive to serve Him better
In all I do and say.

It's also a daily reminder
Of the peace and comfort I share
With all who know my Master
And give themselves to His care.

So, I carry a cross in my pocket,
Reminding no one but me
That Jesus Christ is the Lord of my life
If only I'll let Him be.

While going home, I walked through the park, and I saw a newborn, perhaps two weeks old. I thought to myself, "Lives end and new lives begin." I then saw two lovers kissing and holding each other close. Young love. My thoughts then wandered back to my parents' old photograph books. I remembered seeing photos of them in this very same park years and years ago—that would have been in the early stages of their relationship.

I looked up at the trees, imagining how they must have grown through every kind of weather, yet today they towered over the same place where my parents' young love once blossomed. The trees had weathered adversity—just like the kind we face in life. Remember how far each of us has come: everything we have faced, all the battles we have endured, and all the fears and heartaches we have overcome. Time moves on and stops for no one, and life is a continuous cycle.

On the Sunday before my dad died, Dad and Mom came to our house for dinner. Dad said he was wondering if a robin was making a nest in the Rose of Sharon beside our back deck. After Dad passed, I found a robin making a nest not in the Rose of Sharon but on a wreath on our front door. This was the door where he had made his final departure from my home. I will never look at a robin the same way again. It will remind me of endings and beginnings and the symbols of the circle of life all around us.

You may be surprised to know about my dad's other gift. He wrote poetry for over 30 years. He said he did this to collect his thoughts and keep his mind active. He wrote about personal experiences and loved ones. When he finished a poem, he would sit down and retype it on an old manual typewriter and add it to his book of poems.

This was the same typewriter he once used to type out all his medications for his doctors at the hospital. One doctor once asked, "Is this list typed on a typewriter?" Dad laughed and said, "Yes," to which the doctor replied, "I thought all the typewriters were now in the Smithsonian!" Dad had laughed as he told us this—he thought it was very funny.

On the morning of Dad's funeral, it occurred to me why the first song Dad had taught me and used to sing to me as a young child was called *I Had a Dream, Dear.*

He told me a poem once came to him in a *dream,* and it took him a mere 10 minutes to write it down. He called it "A Wake-up Call." His words sum it up better than mine ever could. I read it at the end of Dad's eulogy.

A Wake-up Call
Written By Robert (Bob) Gough

The other night I had quite a fright,
It was only a dream but what a sight.
People were around me, I could hear them crying,
Though it was only a dream, I knew I was dying.

What surprised me, was I didn't care,
I left my body, I was floating in the air.
I had left this world, I was at a great height,
I could see I was travelling towards a bright light.

I arrived at this place surrounded by walls,
The gatekeeper thanked me for answering his call.
He opened a big book and began turning pages,
Looking for dates, for names and the ages.

He was checking rows of columns while he had me
wait,
When he found my name he opened the gate.
The city within was all white and gold,
There were different races of people, some young and
some old.

Of the women and men there, there was a few,
Old friends and co-workers and neighbours I knew.
We would all stay together till a certain date,
We would then be judged and learn our fate.

Those who led a good life would be treated well,
The rest would be cast out to fall into hell.
I'm sorry I opened my eyes at this time,
'Cause I never found out what fate would be mine.

Was this dream a warning allowing me to see,
Where I go in the hereafter will be up to me.

Chapter 23
May We Always Heed the Sound of His Voice

Like a shepherd He feeds His flock. In His arms He gathers the lambs, carrying them in His bosom, and leading the ewes with care.

—Isaiah 40:11

Many of us cannot relate to the analogy of shepherds and sheep, although the Bible refers to Jesus as the Good Shepherd. We, of course are His flock and He watches over us, lest we go astray.

Parents can be shepherds, too. After all, they watch over their children as shepherds look after their sheep. They feed, protect and try to lead their children along a safe path throughout life.

I am reminded of our gentle Father, who watches over us, leads us, feeds us, protects us and guides us. We need Him; it is very easy to lose our way and go astray.

Three months after my dad's passing, and while I was still in the thick of writing this book, my husband and I took a small 10-day vacation in Newfoundland. It was a place John and I had always wanted to visit, and it was the only province we had not yet had the opportunity of visiting, so we looked forward to it with much anticipation for adventure.

We had wanted to make this trip while Dad was still alive, and he'd known we were planning on going. We had all talked about it together some months before our trip. Dad and Mom had visited Newfoundland themselves twice and really had a wonderful experience, and they had fond memories there.

Spiritually, this trip had no significance except for something that happened over the dates of July 2 and July 3, 2013. Isn't that interesting? The numbers two and three again.

We had stayed in a tranquil town called Fortune for the evening, and the next day, on July 2, we boarded the inter-island ferry boat over to the French island of St. Pierre. Now, this wasn't a place Mom and Dad had visited, but it was a place my husband had always wanted to investigate, since he has such an affinity for France and Europe in general.

Since my Dad's passing, it was becoming a common practice for me to ask God in my prayers to show me that Dad was okay and was now safe in His care.

On the morning of July 2, I dreamed about Dad for the first time since his passing. God had answered my prayer. I saw Dad, and it was like he was beside me, and we were moving together in the same direction, although there was no car or vehicle; we were alongside each other, and we were both moving forward together at the same speed.

I noticed he wasn't wearing his glasses, and something was different, but I didn't quite know at the time what it was. I smiled at Dad and said to him, "Dad, are you all right?"

He looked at me and said, "I'm perfectly fine."

I could tell he was more than fine, as I could feel this peaceful aura around us. It was not an aura I could see, but it was an aura I could feel radiating perfect peace.

"Do you miss me?" I asked.

"They are keeping me really busy," he said.

There was something different, too. The words he spoke to me were spoken mind to mind, not through words as we know it. The closest word in English for this phenomenon would be *telepathy*, but that would leave out the knowledge of emotions.

The only other message Dad gave me was "I'm here to take you where you need to go."

At the time, I felt unsure what that exactly meant, but as I looked at Dad, I could see something different, and it was then my eyes opened and I was awake. My husband now entered the room. He had awoken before me and had gone to find his morning coffee. I looked at him and said, "I just saw Dad in a dream, and he talked to me. His face was flawless. He didn't have any age spots anymore. They were all gone."

Dad had lived to age 84, and the world had left its mark on him, but he always kept his humour. ("When you get old, you start to look like leopard," he told me once.) That comment still makes me smile.

John wasn't surprised at the change. "That's because you saw his Heavenly face" was his reply.

Hours after my dream, we left Fortune for the island of St. Pierre to spend an afternoon and evening there. We ventured out that day and had dinner in a nice French restaurant. Nothing too eventful happened until the next day.

In the morning, we took the ferry boat back, as we had plans to drive to Cape St. Mary's, an Ecological Reserve located at the southwestern tip of the Avalon Peninsula. This was the one place I had planned to visit. From their photographs, I knew my parents visited there, and my Dad had fallen in love with this place. Until this day, I hadn't understood why. (Later, I also found out the *Titanic* sank about 400 miles [640 kilometres] off this coast in the vicinity of this place. How strange when I learned my grandmother could have been a part of that tragedy which happened over 100 years ago and history would have rewritten every line.

The cape shore scenic drive meanders through dense woods and bare hills before emerging onto one of the world's most southerly expanses of sub-Arctic tundra. Cape St. Mary's is one of the most spectacular and accessible seabird observation sites in the world. It is a rare gem that juts into the waters of the north-west Atlantic. It is unique among Newfoundland seabird colonies in being the only one not situated on an offshore island. The colony extends along precipitous coastal cliffs for more than five kilometres and includes well over 50,000 seabirds. You can drive within 1 kilometre of the main nesting location and walk to a viewpoint only 10 to 20 metres from active nests. No location in eastern North America offers a more intimate view of the courtship, nesting and rearing behaviour of Northern Gannets, Black-legged Kittiwakes, and Common and Thick-billed Murres.

After we walked the treeless plateau—which was clad in mosses, lichens, alpine wildflowers, low-growing shrubs, tough grasses, and spongy sphagnum peat and was scattered with boulders abandoned by glaciers in the last Ice Age—we arrived at the closest viewpoint. The throngs of the birds filled the air with strident cries and the pungent scents of their natural habitat.

As I looked around, I could see white sheep at the edge of the barrens, as the land plunged down steep slopes and sheer cliffs to the sea. Through the mist, you could see the waves crashing along the rugged coast down below. In front of me stood the massive 100-metre-high sea stack known as "Bird Rock." It was covered with seabirds.

As I stood there, I remembered the message in my vision the day before: "I'm here to take you where you need to go." It was there that I felt close to life as we know it, to my Dad and to God. Sheep and lambs and all! It was here I reached into my camera bag and pulled out two photographs. They had been taken of each of my parents at this place.

I looked at the markings on the rocks in the pictures, and I realized my father had not been scared of heights! As I trembled, I moved to the place where Dad had sat, and as I held up the photograph of this special man, my husband took the memorial photograph. I did the same with my mother's photo. It was one of the most moving moments of my life. I realized you don't say goodbye to them at the time they pass away; you say goodbye at every crossroad, every milestone, and every big—or little—event that occurs, for true love touches every part of the innermost soul.

I couldn't tell you what time it was, or how long we spent there, but time sure seemed to stand still. Time seemed irrelevant, not real. As in my visions, time seemed to be absent. Is time only created on earth? Is darkness only the lack of light and is cold only the lack of heat? Without clocks, would your life just go on?

This was just how I imagined time to be like in Heaven. We let the moment fill all our senses. The mist obscured my vision, and yet things had never been clearer.

Life is simpler than we make it. Loved ones and other people and animals are precious creatures. We have the wonderful privilege to spend our short time on Earth with these wonderful entities.

When we began our hike back, we were both deep in thought, and words were few. John then said to me, "It wasn't until you took those photographs out and held them up that I realized why you wanted to come here. I found I could hardly take the photos of you. I was feeling emotionally moved in the moment."

It was a special moment I'll never forget.

I had one more task. I needed to determine if "I'm here to take you where you need to go" meant to the bird sanctuary itself or if it meant something different or someplace throughout my life. I suppose I shall eventually find out. Isn't life exciting! But what I do know is Dad is still with me, and he continues to live within my heart each day, everywhere I go.

It wasn't until we returned home, three weeks later on the day of July **23**, **2013**, that the sequence of dates came to mind for me. I found an article which brought clarity to the significance of this place. This is what the article said: "The first known European visitors to Cape St. Mary's were Basque and Portuguese mariners who came to fish in the productive waters around its headlands. An early name for the site was Cabo de Tormenta (Cape of Tempests), but by 1536 it had been renamed Cabo de Santa Maria, in honour of the Virgin Mary, patron saint of Portugal and, doubtless, a source of hope for many a storm-tossed sailor."

Strange as it seems, it wasn't until the morning of July 3, 2014—a year after we were there, on the same date—that Dad's words came through to me again like I cannot describe: "I'm here to take you where you need to go."

The day I completed writing this book I told my guiding light, my mother. She was thrilled to hear I had dedicated it to Dad and that it was finally complete. In her words, "He already knows, and if I know him, he's already read it." (He was an avid book reader.) Then I remembered how his death had triggered all the chapters and inspiration for this book's start. Did the vision mean to write this book? After all, everything is in God's timing!

Then I was also reminded of my friend from the East Coast, whom I talked about earlier. This was the friend with whom I shared a two-hour conversation on the grass at the cemetery near our dearly departed friend. She had said to me then, "I just love your photography and the places you take us. I hope you haven't given up on the idea of publishing a coffee table book of all your cherished photographs Kate. You really must share your other God-given gift." Was that what Dad meant? Was that where I needed to go from here? What a perfect name, "God-Given Gifts." After all, photography is also about light! In 1911, newspaper editor Arthur Brisbane first coined the phrase, "Use a picture. It's worth a thousand words." This sermon is yet to be written.

My final thought is this: Please pray for me, as I feel I was destined to write this book, for I believe books are the mirrors of the soul. The year I started this book was 2013, which had been proclaimed the Year of Faith.

Storms will continue to occur in this world, and in each of our lives, but with those storms come spiritual growth and understanding within ourselves. How incredible it would be if we would begin to see more of the light that exists in ourselves and in each other, for we are called to be light-givers—giving light to others.

There's an old expression, "You can't give what you don't have." If we don't have the light of Christ in us, then that light cannot shine out of us. But when we do have that light of Christ burning brightly in us, it cannot help but shine out of us, showing others His love and throwing off the guiding light of encouragement as a symbol of hope to those in darkness. He is the centre of everything.

Know with certainty a peace that is real, because with God, peace always prevails. Hope is "the muscle of faith." Faith and hope are only needed in this world. Only love prevails in Heaven.

I pray you open your heart, reading my words, and discover His Love and this Light, whether today finds you in sunshine or storm. You see, it doesn't matter how near or far you may be from God today. You can always get closer. He's always waiting with open arms.

Final Thoughts

*The way I see it, our natural human instinct
is to fight or flee that which we perceive to be
dangerous. Although this mechanism evolved to
protect us, it serves as the single greatest limit-
ing process to our growth. To put this process in
perspective and not let it rule my life, I expect the
unexpected; make the unfamiliar familiar; make
the unknown known; make the uncomfortable
comfortable; believe the unbelievable.*

— Charles F. Glassman, MD

In that ambulance on November 11, 2014, on my way to
the hospital, all I could think of was "I can't die yet. My
book needs to be completed and shared with the world."

In February 2015, my husband and I took an enjoyable
cruise that included travelling 80 kilometres between the
Pacific and Atlantic Oceans through the Panama Canal.
This waterway is cut through one of the narrowest saddles
of the isthmus that joins North and South America. The
canal uses a system of locks to carry ships up and over
the divide.

Our cruise ship entered from the Pacific and exited into
the Atlantic. Ships from all parts of the world transit daily

through the Panama Canal, and the canal provides transit service to vessels of all nations without discrimination. As I watched the last lock close, I stood in the hot sun, with my camera perched to take photographs. I stared at the last lock number as our boat entered. Only seconds before, I'd had one of the strangest of moments. I actually thought about this book, and for one split second, I felt that closure would come.

As our cruise ship entered and the final lock closed, I noticed the number **13** painted on the last lock door. I had been told there would have been 4,000 people, including passengers and staff, aboard that day. As I stood there, focusing my lens on the number **13** painted on the last lock door, I started to wonder how many of those 4,000 passengers also noticed this number **13**. When I saw the **13**, I knew I was right where I was supposed to be yet again. And as the final lock closed, I recall having a bizarre visual experience that convinced me to carefully observe this sign and pay close attention to this powerful parallel. It was foreshadowing the closure for my book!

Three weeks later, on the morning of March 8, 2015, I opened my eyes, and I announced this book's content was complete (except for more editing).

My husband looked at me and said, "Well, that is interesting."

I asked, "What do you mean?"

He said, "Of course your book is complete today. For today is the only day in the year that has **23** hours; for it is the day we move the clocks ahead as we transition into Daylight Savings Time. When else would it be complete?" I gave him a frozen stare.

A few days later, it also struck me it was **23** months since my dear father had passed away. The grace of the angels who have guided me through this process to deliver these messages to you, have been perfectly miraculous, and as I said before, "Everything is all in His timing."

On June 3, 2015, I was in St. Patrick's Cathedral in Belfast, Ireland. I had just talked to my publisher, days before leaving home, and had spent the last week surrounded by sheep once again, only this time in the beautiful Irish countryside.

As I knelt down to ask God to lead me through the fire and keep guiding me as I brought these words to print, a bright ray of sunshine shone directly on me through the stained glass window from the back of the church. Never in my life had I seen or felt such a concentration of light in response to my prayer. I looked from my praying hands up to the light that was shining on only a few pews around us. My eyes widened as I looked around at this intense light that surrounded only us. I felt this was a sign from God. I whispered to my husband, "Is this really happening?"

In our smallness but God's greatness, isn't it nice to know that there are devoted angels that surround us and confirm our messages, no matter what.

If you have read my stories and find yourself at this last page, I just want to say this: When I started out to write this book, I felt the Holy Spirit gently nudging me onward, encouraging me to commit to it, to stay true and to follow through to its completion. It's what I was called to do. At the time, I knew I wasn't meant to be a multi-published novelist, and I felt unworthy to fulfill God's call, but I felt I was called to reach out to others for Him, even if I was able to touch only one heart.

I was told my voice may be the only voice able to reach some readers. Others may come close, but my words, for some, will be the exact words they need to read or hear. If these stories never got published, I knew the words I'd written were, at the very least, both a means of recording my visions and a way to heal my own heart. I knew if no one else ever read my words other than hopefully my children and my grandchildren, I'd still be thrilled to have been able to record these words for them. I pushed onward, committing myself to finishing the book, knowing it may never get published in the traditional way.

If it made it into your hands—you, a perfect stranger— and if you had an open mind and learned something, may God bless you. I thank you.

I have placed my trust in Him; He gave me the words.

My child, God is everywhere. Each of us is unique because that is the gift given to each person by God. May God bless you in ways you never even dreamed possible and from every corner of the world. Stay bright in God's grace, and may the blessings of each day be the blessings you need most.

I leave you with an Irish Celtic Parable called "Grasping Water":

> *You cannot grasp water in your hand.*
> *It drops through your fingers.*
>
> *You cannot grasp truth in your mind.*
> *It drops through your thoughts.*
>
> *You can only possess water by drinking it.*
> *Taking it into your body.*
>
> *You can only possess truth by living it.*
> *Taking it into your heart.*

Photographs

One day an old photograph may be all that is left

As proof that you and I were ever here.

A happy life, a sad one—it will matter then only to you.

So make the most out of your life today,

And live it for those you love, and live it for you,

As other than the love you shared,

An old photograph may be all that is

left when your life is through.

July 1959 – Little Beach, Port Stanley, Ontario
Kate, Dad & brother Robert Jr.

January 1963 – Winter at Home
Mom, Kate and Rebel #1

July 1964 – Ipperwash Beach
Kate & her brother Robert Jr. & Rebel #2

January 1965 – Dad's Skating Rink
Kate & her brother Robert Jr.

1966 – Niagara Falls, Ontario Family Photo
Robert Jr., Mom, Dad & Kate

1967 – Dress Up Days
Kate with childhood & life time friend, Carla

**December 1966 – Chicken Pox on Christmas Day
Kate & Grandfather, Herbert Gough (Papa)**

July 1969 – Kate & Timmy, my grandfather's dog

1975 – Kate & Grandmother, Rose (Nona)

2002 – My father gave me my first camera at age 10. Later this became "Kate's Captures" (my photography company) and one of my greatest gifts!

July 11, 2012 – 65th Wedding Anniversary
Mom & Dad

July 2015 – Kate & Mother, Ann

2008 – Our Hyland Family Photo

2015 – Our Hyland Family Photo, give or take a few...

2011 – Christmas Day
Matthew, Mom, Dad, Kate, Nike & John

1994 – My Danish Family in Canada

2007 – My Danish Family in Denmark
Bent, Kate & Bente

2008 –My "Happy Childhood Place"
Kate (pre-cancer) at Ipperwash Beach

2009 – Kate's Cancer Journey Painting

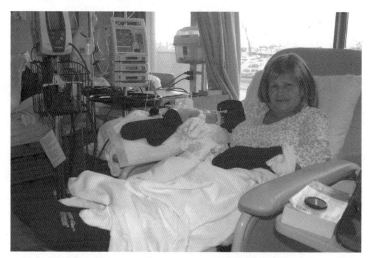

February to May 2010 – 18 Weeks of Chemotherapy Treatment

2009 – Kate & Nike together in the Cancer Journey

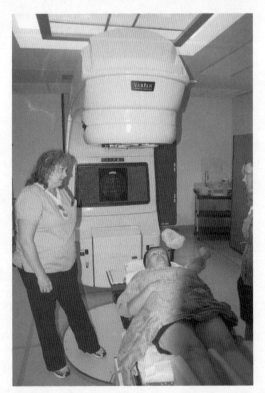

July to August 2010 – Five weeks of Daily Radiation

2010 - Nike & My "Pink Ribbon" Cancer Journey

2011 – Summer Picnic
Kate, Mom & Dad wearing his "Believe" hat

August 2010 – BEFORE "The Accident"

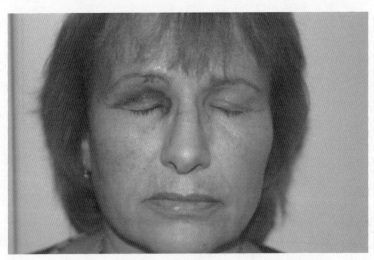

August 2010 – AFTER "The Accident"

June 2012 – Cancer Relay Event, St. Thomas, Ontario
My "Survivor Sisters" Maria, Judy, Kate & Lori)

October 2014 – Run for the Cure, London, Ontario

June 2012 – Baltic Trip with The Smith's in Russia
Brian, Janet, Tour Guide, Kate & John

June 2012 – #13
You are right where you are supposed to be! ...in Norway

November 2012 – Kate at Wailing Wall in Jerusalem, Israel

Nike's "Swoosh"

Spring 2012 – Keeping the Hope Alive
Nike & my daffodils

June 2013 – Newfoundland, Canada
Kate holding the picture of her father at "Bird Rock"

October 2013 – Kate on Omaha Beach, Normandy, France

My Praying Place

February 23, 2014
Friend, Debbie & Karen's "Angel Wings"

2014 – My husband John, "My Rock" for over 30 years

February 2015 – Panama Locks Closing (Final Thoughts)

February 2015 – Panama Locks #13 (Final Thoughts)

Printed in Canada